EUGENE BULLARD

EUGENE BULLARD

World's First Black Fighter Pilot

LARRY W. GREENLY

NEWSOUTH BOOKS
Montgomery

NewSouth Books
105 S. Court Street
Montgomery, AL 36104

Library of Congress Cataloging-in-Publication Data

Greenly, Larry W.
Eugene Bullard : world's first Black fighter pilot / Larry W. Greenly.
pages cm
Includes bibliographical references.

ISBN 978-1-58838-280-1 (hardcover)
ISBN 978-1-60306-196-4 (ebook)

1. Bullard, Eugene Jacques, 1894-1961. 2. African American fighter
pilots—France—Biography. 3. Fighter pilots—France—Biography. 4.
African American fighter pilots—Biography. 5. World War, 1914–
1918—Aerial operations, French. 6. World War, 1939-1945—Aerial
operations, French. 7. Race discrimination—United States—History—
20th century. I. Title.

TL540.B747G74 2012
940.4944092—dc23
[B]
2012036425

Design by Randall Williams
Printed in the United States of America

For Edith,
my wife of many years, who made this book
(and many other things in my life) possible

Contents

Preface

Several years ago, I wanted to write a biography of someone who had ties to the Southwest. While actively searching for someone interesting, I happened to watch the movie *Flyboys* (2006). Even though *Flyboys* was an exciting film to watch, it had a number of historical and technical inaccuracies, particularly the conflating of the Lafayette Escadrille with the Lafayette Flying Corps. Confusion still exists between those two units with similar names, but more about that later.

I first zeroed in on one of the pilots, Blaine Rawlings, who was from Texas (at least in the film). Rawlings's character was based on the real-life World War I ace, Frank Luke, who was born in Arizona. Then I noticed the black character, Eugene Skinner, who was a boxer before he became a pilot for France. Skinner was loosely based on Eugene Bullard from Georgia, who is the subject of this book.

When I did a little research on Eugene Bullard, I found that he was a particularly interesting person but not very well known. A search of Albuquerque's library system using Bullard's name turned up a rare copy of *The Black Swallow of Death* by P. J. Carisella and James W. Ryan. The book consisted of Bullard's memoirs, which he wrote in the latter years of his life, as well as interviews of Bullard's associates by Carisella and Ryan.

The Black Swallow of Death literally changed my life. After reading it, I couldn't forget the outrageously colorful life that Bullard had led. Here was a story that deserved to be told, a story of a courageous black man who grew up poor in America and later became a highly decorated World War I soldier and pilot in France. Yet when he returned to the United States, he suffered prejudices until he died in relative obscurity. I researched Bullard further and obtained much of my information from the books listed in "Further Reading," particularly *The Black Swallow of Death*; *Eugene Bullard: Expatriate in Jazz-Age Paris*; and *The Lafayette Flying Corps*, Vols. 1 and 2.

This book is a narrative biography: facts—such as people, dates, places, and activities—are as accurate as possible, but the dialogue is mostly fabricated. A narrative biography strives to turn a mundane compilation of facts into an exciting book for readers to enjoy. There is no doubt that Bullard misremembered some of his exploits or even exaggerated them in his memoirs, but I chose the facts the best I could from among various sources. On occasion, I may have used an exaggeration from Bullard himself, but I was always cautious to make sure the essence of his story remained true.

AS MENTIONED ABOVE, MANY contemporary readers are confused by the similar names of the Lafayette Escadrille and the Lafayette Flying Corps. Such confusion is no doubt compounded by the *Flyboys* movie and other sources. The difference between the two units are:

The French Service Aéronautique was the overall French Air

Force. The Escadrille Américaine, a subordinate component of the Service Aéronautique, was formed to allow American pilots to fly and fight for France. The Franco-American Corps, also a subordinate component of the French Service Aéronautique, was formed to allow both French and American pilots to fly together.

Germany complained to France that the United States was neutral at that time and that Americans flying against Germany was a diplomatic violation. As a consequence, France removed the reference to Americans flying for France by renaming the Escadrille Américaine to the Escadrille Lafayette. Soon after, France renamed the Franco-American Corps to the Lafayette Flying Corps for the same reason.

Eugene Bullard flew for the Lafayette Flying Corps, not the Lafayette Escadrille. He was a truly remarkable man. I hope this book will inspire others to celebrate his life and remember him as an American hero.

First and foremost, I'd like to thank my critique group, Rob Spiegel, Sue Houser, Wendy Bickel, and Jacqueline Bickel, for their endless encouragement and their tireless support in making my manuscript the best it could be.

I'd be remiss in not mentioning SouthWest Writers, one of the most supportive writing organizations in the country. As a long-time member, I have learned about writing over the years from some of the best writers in the country.

I found Brett Stolle in the United States Air Force National Museum, Research Division, to be a lifesaver when I desperately needed high-resolution images of Eugene Bullard. I also owe Kathy Kitts a debt of gratitude for the French pronunciation guide included in this book.

And I can never repay those other writers who believed in this book enough to write cover blurbs—especially my friend, David Morrell.

SOURCES OF ILLUSTRATIONS

Pages 2, 29, 37, 40, 59, 63, 76, 79, 82, 83, 88, 89, 112, 132, 133, 137: courtesy of the National Museum of the U.S. Air Force in Dayton, Ohio.

Pages 65, 71, 73, 85: from *The Lafayette Flying Corps* by Charles Nordhoff (now in the public domain).

Page 98: from http://www.airwar.ru/enc/fww1/pfd3.html (public domain).

Page 134: the photo was taken at the National Museum of the U.S. Air Force by, and is used courtesy of, Flickr user OZinOH.

EUGENE BULLARD

Eugene Bullard, shown here in his French aviators'
uniform, was a member of the French Foreign Legion and
flew with the French Lafayette Corps.

Prologue

Lucky

Eugene Bullard struggled to keep his sputtering biplane from crashing. He headed back toward French-occupied territory. Tracer bullets from machine guns in the trenches below streaked around him. Thwack, thwack, thwack! A line of holes marched across a lower wing.

Splang! One bullet punched through the front cowling. The SPAD's engine belched black smoke. Sweet-smelling castor oil sprayed Bullard's windshield and face. He wiped his goggles with his sleeve and desperately worked his throttle to keep the engine running.

It seemed like every German soldier in the trenches below was firing at him while Bullard coaxed his sputtering plane over the enemy lines. The SPAD's engine gasped one last time and died. Bullard had no choice now. He had to land—in a plane that glided like a brick.

A muddy field in no-man's land appeared ahead. Wind whistled past Bullard's falling plane. Pushing away fear, he focused on landing. He tore off his goggles; they might shatter on impact. The ground came up fast. Bullard held his breath. *Don't stall, keep the wings level, don't hit a shellhole*. He carefully pulled back on his stick. The SPAD's wheels hit ground. The plane bounced, bounced, bounced and finally came to rest.

Bullard exhaled. *At least I didn't flip over.* Machine-gun bullets drilled the air around the downed SPAD. Bullard unfastened his seat belt, clambered over the far side of his fuselage, and fell into a muddy crater. As long as the Germans were firing at him, he could only lie in the cold mud and listen to bullets puncturing his plane.

Hours dragged by. He shivered in his soaking wet clothes. As darkness settled over no-man's land, the constant sniping at Bullard finally ended. Should he run for it?

Without warning, voices emerged from a shell-destroyed forest behind him. Bullard whirled around. With a sigh of relief, he realized they were speaking French.

"Ah, Monsieur Bullard, I see you are still alive." It was Bullard's aircraft mechanic. "We are here to transport your pathetic airplane back for repair."

A group of mechanics and soldiers appeared out of the shadows. The men quickly dragged Bullard's plane to a safe area out of sight. In no time, the mechanics had the SPAD's wings removed. They lifted the fuselage onto a flat transport wagon hitched to two horses, loaded the wings and tied everything down. Bullard and the men hopped into the back of a truck. They headed for the airfield a few miles away.

"I counted 96 holes in your machine, Bullard," the mechanic said. "None in you. You're a lucky man."

Yes, lucky. Bullard reflected on that. *How did a black Georgia boy like me wind up flying for the French Lafayette Corps?*

1

Childhood

Stewart County, Georgia

In 1863, Eugene's father, William Octave Bullard, was born to a slave family on a Georgia cotton plantation. The tiny black infant was named after Wiley Bullard, the owner and master of that plantation on the Chattahoochee River about 40 miles south of Columbus, Georgia. After slaves were freed when the Civil War ended in 1865, Octave and his parents had nowhere to go, so they kept working for Wiley Bullard. Octave grew to six-feet, four-inches tall and 250 pounds of solid muscle—which made him an incredibly strong and useful field hand.

When Octave reached 19 in 1882, he decided to marry a 17-year-old Creek Indian girl named Josephine and strike out on his own. Soon afterward, Octave and Josephine Bullard moved to Columbus and rented a cabin. W. C. Bradley, a white businessman, appreciated Bullard's obvious strength and hired him as a stevedore unloading boats at his cotton warehouse. Bullard was a hard worker and almost everyone liked him, especially Mr. Bradley. He nicknamed Bullard "Big Chief Ox" partly because of his name, partly because of his strength, and partly because of his marriage to an Indian.

Over the next 12 years, the Bullard family grew to 10 children. On October 9, 1895, Eugene James Bullard, Octave and Josephine's seventh child, was born.

When Eugene was growing up, he loved everyone. He enjoyed playing with the neighborhood children. And he loved riding around the nearby streets in his goat-drawn cart. But for some reason, his mother wouldn't let him play with white children. After his mother died when he was almost seven years old, he found out why. He tried playing with the white neighbors, but they would taunt him and call him names.

Eugene would forget about the name-calling, though, when his father told his family wonderful stories about the Bullard family and distant lands. Eugene's favorite stories were about France, a place far, far away—across the Atlantic Ocean.

"In France," Mr. Bullard told them, "slavery was abolished many years ago. And blacks are treated as well as whites. Someday I'll take you there so you can see for yourself."

One evening, Mr. Bullard told the older children about some problems he was having on the job. A man named Stevens, who supervised Mr. Bradley's warehouse, didn't like blacks. He cursed at blacks and hit and kicked them. "And he's jealous of me because Mr. Bradley likes me so much."

A few weeks later, Bullard was working in the cotton warehouse and standing near a loading hole in the floor. Stevens came up behind him and started cursing him. Bullard didn't say anything, which made Stevens more angry. He cursed even louder. Bullard still didn't say anything.

"I'll kill you!" the red-faced Stevens shouted. He grabbed an iron loading hook, swung around and smashed Bullard on the side of his head.

RD

d." He carefully shut the

that night. Early the next
d their father stepped in.
hooped with delight and
ey could.

u while I was gone?" Mr.

radley was real good to us.
here is."

knee and cupped Eugene's
ve different color skins, and
." He brushed his hand on
everyone right—no matter
ct you."

ite person," Eugene retorted.
here are probably millions of
orld. I know that in France,
te to black folks." He stood
so you can see for yourself."
sed for the summer. Eugene
months. At night he couldn't
hable to get France out of his
place where everyone treated

k for France, he thought one
r money?

had a plan: he would sell his
, he led his goat across a nearby
it to the owner's son for $1.50.

The blow almost knocked him over. But despite the blood pouring from the terrible gash on his head, Bullard remained on his feet. He felt his head and stared at his hands, covered in blood. Then he looked up at Stevens, who looked shocked that Eugene's father was still standing.

The enraged Bullard grabbed Stevens by both arms, lifted him overhead and threw him headfirst through the floor hole into the storage hold below. Stevens landed with a sickening thud. Not even a moan came out of the hold.

Still bleeding and holding his head, Bullard ran to Mr. Bradley's office. After hearing the story, Bradley knew that Bullard might be lynched for what he had done to a white man—particularly if Stevens died. Bradley bandaged Bullard's head, and they both walked back to the warehouse to find Stevens.

Luckily, they discovered that Stevens was badly injured but still alive. Bradley advised Bullard to hide until nightfall for his own safety. It wasn't long before an angry crowd appeared at the warehouse. Bradley tried to convince them that Stevens had tripped and fallen into the hold, but the crowd's grumblings showed they didn't believe it.

Bullard sneaked home after dark, locked the door and told his frightened children to go to bed and to keep quiet. At midnight, sudden pounding on the front door and loud cursing from outside broke the family's tense silence. Bullard peeked out a window and saw a white, drunken mob, some of whom were passing around bottles of liquor.

"Are you in there, Ox?" voices yelled. "Come on out." The pounding continued. Someone yelled for an axe to break down the door. "Ah, he's probably not here," someone else said. "He'd be crazy to come home."

After more arguing and drinking and pounding on t[h]
door, the mob decided Bullard wasn't home and finally lef[t]

"Children," Mr. Bullard finally said. "Promise you won['t]
mention a word of this to anyone, no matter what." He kisse[d]
his shaken children. "I'm going to leave for a while."

With that, he quietly slipped out the door into the darkness.

LEAVING HOME

For two days, the Bullard children wondered where their
father was hiding—or if he were even alive. They were also
afraid the mob that pounded on their door two nights ago
might have lynched their father for fighting with his white
supervisor.

On the second evening after their father had left, the children heard a wagon pull up to their front door. The oldest girl,
Pauline, peeked out. Albert, a black man, was driving a wagon
owned by Mr. Bradley. Pauline swung open the door for him.

"Good evening, Miss Bullard," Albert said, handing her
an envelope. "I have a letter from Mr. Bradley."

Pauline tore open the envelope and read the contents to
the other children:

> Your father is all right, and he is in no danger. Keep
> going to school as if nothing has happened. And if you
> need any money or food or anything else, just let Albert
> know, and I'll get it to you. — W. C. Bradley

Every night they prayed and sang hymns before bedtime,

ten him a job working for the railro[ad]
door behind him.

The children could hardly sleep
morning, the door swung open, a[nd]
Eugene and the other children w[ere]
hugged their father as tightly as th[ey]

"How did Mr. Bradley treat y[ou]
Bullard asked.

Eugene answered first. "Mr. B[radley]
He's the only good white person

Mr. Bullard got down on his
chin in his huge hand. "People ha[ve]
some are good and some are bad
Eugene's hair. "Respect and treat
what color—or they won't respe[ct]

"Well, I only know one nice wh[ite]

"Hmm," Mr. Bullard said. "T[here are]
nice white people around the w[orld]
white people are nice and poli[te]
up. "Someday I'll take you ther[e]

June arrived and school clo[sed]
would be 11 years old in a few
sleep. He tossed and turned, u[nable to]
mind and dreaming about a
everyone else with respect .

Maybe I could leave and lo[ok]
night. But what would I do fo[r]

The next morning, Eugen[e]
goat and find France. At sunse[t]
field to a lumberyard and sold

Eugene remembered a gypsy camp across the railroad tracks and figured it would be a good hideout from his father until the next morning. He headed for their campfire .

"Who are you?" the gypsies asked when Eugene appeared.

"Oh, I been visitin' some relatives, and I'm goin' back home." Eugene replied.

An old gypsy lady handed Eugene a bucket. "Fetch some water for our horses."

When Eugene came back from the creek, the old lady handed him a plate of food. After Eugene finished his meal, he saw his angry father heading toward the camp. He quickly hid underneath one of the painted gypsy wagons.

"Did you see a boy with a goat?" Mr. Bullard gruffly asked the gypsies.

The gypsies looked at each other. "No such boy around here."

At sunrise, Eugene awoke and walked through some woods to a railroad track. He was on his way to France.

2

Journey

On the Road

Eugene didn't dare walk along dirt roads. Any farmer driving his wagon to market might recognize him and tell his father. Eugene headed toward the rising sun and walked on the railroad ties, counting them as they passed under him. He thought about his father's words: "In France, everyone is treated the same" and "a Bullard never gives up."

As the day got warmer, the ties oozed sticky creosote, and its strong smell filled the air. Occasionally, Eugene walked on top of a rail, balancing himself with his arms out on each side. When he tired of that, he crunched alongside the tracks on the gravel bed, always heading toward what he hoped was France.

After walking all day on the tracks through lonely stretches of woods, Eugene hadn't seen another person, but his legs and feet were getting tired. As dusk fell, his imagination took over. He'd heard of people getting murdered at night on railroad tracks. He shivered. And what about bears looking for food? He hurried his pace, looking for a dirt road so he could leave the tracks.

Stars emerged in the darkening sky. Eugene forgot about his tired legs and ran until he finally found a dirt road crossing. Relief washed over him, but a new worry soon arose. He thought everyone knew his secret—that he was a runaway.

He tried to avoid people and keep on the move so he wouldn't look suspicious. But near the crossing he met Tom and Emma, black sharecroppers with 13 children, who took him in for the night. When the family arose early to work the next day, Emma handed Eugene a dollar bill and wished him well on his journey.

That morning, Eugene headed for the nearest station where a few people were waiting for the train. If he bought a ticket himself, Eugene thought, the station agent might recognize him and tell his father.

Eugene got up his courage and approached a friendly looking white man. "How much is a half-fare to Atlanta?"

"A dollar."

Eugene handed the man a dollar and asked him to please buy a ticket.

Holding his newly purchased ticket, Eugene trembled a bit when he saw the headlights of the train approaching the station. Someone on the train might recognize him. Maybe his father was on the train. He clambered on board, not looking at anyone.

He sat next to a plump black woman, the widow Mary Wood, who struck up a conversation. By the time they reached Atlanta, Mrs. Wood had convinced Eugene to stay overnight with her. The next morning, the widow urged Eugene to stay longer because she had no family and was very lonely.

"But I'm on my way to France," Eugene said. "And you're so kind, if I stay with you, I'll never want to leave."

After saying his goodbyes to Mrs. Wood, Eugene walked

back to the Atlanta train station. But he was too afraid to buy a ticket. His father might be inside. He hurried away and was soon lost in the nearby stockyards.

A young white man noticed Eugene and approached him. "Hey, kid! How would you like to travel with us for a year? You'd get a dollar a week for taking care of our horses and mules."

Eugene could tell the young man was a gypsy. He knew gypsies treated everyone alike, and he knew they traveled a lot. Maybe even to France. "Do you ever go to France?" he asked.

"Sure we do," the gypsy said. "We travel all over the world."

Eugene couldn't believe his luck. "When do I start?"

The next morning, Eugene showed up at the stockyard and met Levy Stanley, the leader of the gypsy band, who was trading some horses. That night Stanley took Eugene to the gypsy camp, fed him and gave him a place to sleep.

The gypsies taught Eugene how to care for horses—how to ride them and how to make them look younger with homemade medications so they would sell for a higher price.

After a while, Eugene approached the gypsy. "When are we going to travel to other countries—like France—where everyone is treated the same?"

"Well," Stanley said, rubbing his chin. "It'll be another two years before we go back to Europe."

That seemed like an eternity to Eugene. The gypsies had treated him well, but it was time to leave his new friends. He'd have to find France on his own.

To the Sea

Eugene walked along a dusty road, hoping he was headed for France even though he didn't really know which way to go. He heard hoofbeats behind him and the rattle of buggy wheels. He stepped to the side of the road.

"Whoa." A white man drew up his horse and buggy next to Eugene. "Hey, boy. You want a ride?"

"Why, thank you, sir." Eugene hopped on board, thinking that his father was right. Not all white people were bad. "I'm on my way to France."

The man smiled. "I'm Travis Moreland." He flicked his whip, and the buggy moved forward. "How 'bout you rest up at my house tonight? I'll give you somethin' to eat. And you can sleep in the corn crib."

The next morning, Eugene was up with the roosters, waiting for Mr. Moreland to appear, so he could say thanks for the hospitality and be on his way. When Moreland showed up, Eugene said his thanks and that he'd be leaving.

"Boy, you don't even know where you're goin'," Moreland said. "Furthermore, I ain't even gonna let you go."

"You can't stop me, sir," Eugene replied. "I'm on my way to France where everyone's treated with respect."

"Don't talk back to me, boy. If you leave, I'll hunt you down. Do whatever the missus wants you to do, and go pump some water for my horses and rub them down."

When Eugene didn't immediately move, Moreland cursed at him. Eugene winced at some of the names the man called him. But Eugene figured if he worked hard all day, Moreland would think that he had forgotten about going to France. Then Moreland wouldn't watch him as closely. Eugene knew he would leave the minute there was a chance to escape.

As the sun set, Moreland sat on a chair on his porch and called to Eugene. And called again. "Why don't you answer me, boy?"

Eugene approached the porch. "You and your wife said I worked well, but you called me nasty names. I'm not staying where people call me names."

Moreland looked shocked and walked into his house, muttering to himself. Dejected, Eugene sat on a tree stump. He wondered what to do next.

About an hour later, Moreland came out and walked over to Eugene. "Okay, you still can't leave, but I won't call you names anymore. What do you want me to call you?"

Eugene brightened. "Call me Eugene or Gypsy, sir." He picked up a broom and started sweeping.

"I like your attitude, Gypsy. I'm gonna give you 50 cents a day to work around the farmyard."

It wasn't long before the hard-working Eugene was promoted to houseboy. Then six months later, Mr. Moreland called Eugene into his parlor.

"Sit down, Gypsy, I got something to tell you."

Blacks didn't usually sit down in a white person's parlor, but Eugene did as he was told.

Mr. Moreland continued. "You've worked hard and earned our respect. We like you, but if you want to go away, it's all right with us."

Eugene stayed a little while longer, but one morning he said his goodbyes to the Morelands and struck out on his own once more.

In the tiny Georgia town called Sasser, he met a white barber named Matthews who asked Eugene to work as a helper for him. For several months, Eugene swept the barbershop and did odd jobs.

One day Eugene didn't show up for work. He was lying in bed with a dangerous fever that rose to 105 degrees. Even though Mr. Matthews was very poor, he sent for a doctor and paid for Eugene's treatment.

While Eugene was recuperating, he began wondering if he had been wrong about white people. *Maybe there were good people of all colors.* He'd have to travel more and find out.

When Eugene recovered, he knew he had to set out for France again. Mr. Matthews was sorry to see Eugene go, but wished him well and gave him three dollars to help him on his way.

Eugene reached Dawson City, Georgia, and met the Zacharias Turner family who hired him for two dollars a week to do stable work. Eugene, hoping to throw off anyone looking for him, told the Turners his name was "Gypsy." The Turners bought horses and mules from Texas. They let Eugene break in their new, wild horses when they discovered how well he handled and treated stock.

Eugene was such a natural with horses that the Turners entered him as a jockey in the 1911 Terrell County Fair horserace. He was a sensation. It was very unusual at that time for a black person to ride as a jockey. Eugene, wearing a red and yellow satin jacket, rode his horse easily. He took the lead and thundered over the finish line to win a length-and-a-half in front of the second-place horse.

Even though Eugene became a hero to the area's black people, he didn't let it go to his head. Instead, he thought it was time to get serious about moving on. One night he told Mr. Turner that he wanted to go to France "where all colored folks are treated right by everybody."

Turner was surprised. He thought he treated Eugene so well, he'd given up wanting to travel. "Gypsy," he said, "when you grow up, I'll let you go to France, but not before."

Eugene didn't say anything more. But starting the next day, he hid clothing and extra coins in the barn for use when the time was right. Four months later, he was told to deliver a buckskin pony to a prison farm in St. Andrews Bay, Florida. After he delivered the horse, he bought a ticket on a narrow-gauge train to Montgomery, Alabama.

After more adventures and some menial jobs in Montgomery, Eugene headed back to Atlanta with $16—a sizable sum in those days. He didn't know what direction he should travel to look for France, but he found a Seaboard Air Line Railway passenger train headed for Richmond, Virginia. He guessed Richmond was as good a place as any. At midnight, he hid underneath the dining car on its undercarriage. A whole day later, the train stopped on a bridge near Jamestown, Virginia. Thinking he was close to Richmond, a weary Eugene hopped off.

After working a week or so in Jamestown as a laborer for a black bricklayer to earn more money, he tried to figure out which train was going all the way to Richmond. By pure chance, he hid underneath a Chesapeake & Ohio train that didn't go to Richmond but to Newport News, a seaport on the Atlantic.

When the train finally stopped and the passengers stepped off, Eugene peeked out from underneath the rail car, looking for anyone who might see him. He climbed off his perch and nonchalantly—but carefully—made his way out of the railyard.

The smell of salt air meant one thing to Eugene. He was closer to France. But he needed to find a ship ready to sail, hopefully one that was sailing to the country of his dreams.

He headed toward the glint of the sea.

On His Way

Eugene reached the waterfront on a Saturday. Steamships filled the harbor. He spied one ship that was being loaded. Was that a ship to France?

Hiding behind a barrel, Eugene watched a line of men carrying crates of cabbages onto the steamer. Once he figured out the rhythm of the loading line, he left his hiding spot and inserted himself between two men who didn't seem to notice. The man in front of Eugene bent forward, and a loader placed a heavy crate on his back. Eugene did the same.

After Eugene walked up the gangway with his load, another pair of men removed it and stacked it with the rest of the cabbage crates. Eugene noticed several large bales of cotton on board. When no one was looking, he quickly hid between two bales.

He soon felt the ship get underway, but he had no idea whether or not it was going to France. After a few hours, the ship stopped. Eugene stayed hidden until he heard men moving the crates. He sneaked out to join another line of men who were now unloading the crates of cabbage and stacking them on the dock.

As before, two men lifted a crate onto Eugene's back. He

walked down the gangway with his load and stacked his crate with the others. He hurried away from the dock and soon found himself downtown in a strange city. Was this France? He noticed a black boy leaning on a lamppost.

"Is this France?" Eugene asked.

The black boy stared at Eugene. "It's Norfolk, Virginia, stupid."

"Oh." *I guess I'll have to try again.*

Eugene headed back to the waterfront and spotted a ship with crew members coming ashore for their leave. As each member passed Eugene, he smiled and said hello, but the crew spoke a language he'd never heard before. Eugene asked around and learned the ship was called the *Marta Russ*. And it was sailing on Monday.

Eugene showed up early the next day and hung around the ship, trying to figure out how to get aboard.

"Hey, kid!" a sailor yelled from the ship. "Come here a second."

Eugene ran up the gangway.

The sailor handed Eugene a pail and a note. "Would you run an errand to a bar for me?"

"Yessir!" Eugene answered.

Eugene soon returned with the pail filled with beer and handed it to the sailor.

"Here's a dime, kid."

"Thanks." Eugene turned to leave. *How am I going to get aboard?*

"Hey, kid. Are you hungry?" the sailor asked.

Eugene nodded.

"I'll get you something to eat."

Eugene looked around for a hiding place, but the sailor returned with some bread and cheese before Eugene could move a step.

"Thank you, sir," Eugene said and sat on the deck. While eating his food he noticed a lifeboat that would be the perfect hiding spot. When he finished, Eugene thanked the crew members and left the ship.

Late that night, Eugene sneaked up the ship's gangway. He carried a sack of sandwiches and fried chicken, enough food—he hoped—to last until he arrived in France. Making sure no one was around, he slipped under the lifeboat's cover and fell asleep.

When Eugene awoke, he was on the high seas—far out of sight of land. As days slowly passed, Eugene ate all of his food and drank his only bottle of water. His hunger and thirst grew so unbearable he knew he'd have to make his presence known.

Eugene followed the smell of food. He made his way to the ship's galley and swung open the door, not knowing what to expect.

"Ach du lieber!" cried out an astonished sailor—the same one who had sent Eugene for beer. "What are you doing here?"

"I'm going to France," Eugene replied. "But I'm really hungry and thirsty."

"We're not going to France, and Captain Westphal is going to be very angry," the sailor said. "Here, eat this food first, and I'll tell you what to say to the captain."

Soon Eugene was standing in front of the captain, who didn't look very happy at the sight of a 16-year-old black stowaway. He thrust his scowling face in front of Eugene. "We should throw you overboard and be done with you."

Eugene forgot what he was told to say and blurted, "I think the fish have enough to eat."

The captain straightened up and laughed. "All right, we're stuck with you. But you'll have to work. We have about 18 more days before we land." The captain thought a moment. "Hmm, you can help the boiler crew."

Starting the next morning, Eugene hauled up countless heavy bags of ashes from the ship's engine room and emptied them overboard. Even though he was physically large and strong for his age, the work was exhausting and continued for almost three weeks.

Near the end of the voyage, the captain called for Eugene. "We are going to lay over at Aberdeen, Scotland, before continuing to Hamburg, Germany."

Eugene had no idea where Aberdeen was or—for that matter—where Hamburg was.

The captain frowned and paced with his hands behind his back. "I might keep you on board until we get to Hamburg and then take you back to Norfolk."

"Oh, please, don't do that," cried Eugene. "I don't want to go back. I want to go to France."

The captain's expression softened. "Well, I guess I'll just have to get rid of you somehow in Aberdeen." He bent down and spun the combination lock on a safe. "Maritime law says I have to pay you for the work you've done." The captain removed an envelope and counted out some bills.

Eugene couldn't believe his eyes. He held out his hands and received $25, a huge sum. A commotion from the deck grabbed his attention. The ship was docking. Eugene thanked the captain, shook his hand and ran down the gangplank to Aberdeen.

Eugene looked around. Now I must be closer to France.

ODD JOBS

It didn't take Eugene long to notice there were no black people around. Wandering the streets of Aberdeen, all he saw were white people who stared at him as they walked by.

Eugene approached one Scot reading a newspaper. "Excuse me, sir, but can you tell me where France is?"

The startled Scot dropped his paper. He stared at Eugene for a second before he regained his composure. "Well, laddie," he said with a thick Scottish burr, "France is hundreds of miles away." He pointed south and chuckled. "That way, actually. Across the English Channel."

Eugene had a hard time understanding the man because of his accent, but it appeared there was another stretch of water to cross. He'd have to go to another city farther south and figure out how to get on another ship.

With a bit of his savings, he purchased a train ticket to Glasgow. Upon arriving in the city, Eugene did not see any black people there, either. The Scottish people who met him sometimes addressed him as "Darky," but he soon realized they were not trying to insult him. He liked Glasgow. The people were polite and friendly.

After he found a room to rent, Eugene figured he had enough money—if he was careful—to last about a month. He made friends with a number of boys his own age and bought them candies and other treats. Within two weeks, he had no money left.

An organ grinder playing a hurdy-gurdy on the streets noticed Eugene hanging out with his friends and thought he could make more money with a black partner. Eugene needed money, so it wasn't long before Eugene was dancing and singing for coins.

A few days later an older man approached Eugene. "Hey, Darky, how'd you like to work for us? All you have to do is just keep an eye on things. And the pay is good."

The man was a riverfront gambler who needed lookouts to warn of police raids. Eugene liked his new job working as a lookout the best of all. The pay was good, and the work was easy. Within a few months, he had saved enough money to move even farther south to England—another step closer to France.

One more train trip deposited him in Liverpool, England, home of a large seaport. *Perfect. I can get a job on the docks.* Within a few days, he was lugging heavy slabs of frozen meat off the ships, making about two dollars a day.

As the days passed, Eugene noticed his body was getting stronger and his muscles were getting larger. But after a month of working, he was so exhausted he decided to look for something less strenuous.

Eugene worked a short time as an assistant on a fish wagon, then nabbed a job in an amusement park. On weekends he would stick his head through a hole in a canvas sheet in a booth, and let customers throw soft rubber balls at him. He attracted a lot of business because the crowds had never seen a black person before. Fortunately, Eugene had quick reflexes and most of the balls—even though they were soft—missed him.

Working only on the weekends meant Eugene had time to explore Liverpool and learn the streets. One day he rounded a corner and stopped in front of Chris Baldwin's Gymnasium.

He wondered what was inside and stepped through the front door.

LEARNING TO FIGHT

Eugene shut the door behind him. The smell of sweat permeated the air. Clanks and thumps echoed between the walls. Men were lifting weights, jumping rope and punching heavy bags that hung from the ceiling. In the rear of the gym, a man yelled directions at two other men who were throwing punches at each other and dancing around in a boxing ring. A gong sounded. The men stopped punching, grabbed their towels and clambered over the ropes.

The man who had been yelling at the boxers was Chris Baldwin—the owner. He spied Eugene standing with his mouth agape. "You come to join us, young man?"

"I was just looking around, sir," Eugene replied. "I wasn't sure what was in here."

Baldwin stood in front of Eugene and wiped his forehead with his sleeve. "We train championship boxers." He looked at Eugene carefully as if measuring him. "Hmm. Average height. A little scrawny. How old are you?"

"Sixteen, sir."

"Maybe if you'd hang around, we could show you how to become a boxer." Baldwin flexed his arms to show off his muscles. "Lemme see you do that."

Eugene held up his arms, flexing them as hard as he could to make his teenage muscles bulge.

"Hmm," Baldwin said. "Not bad, but if you're gonna be a boxer . . . you do want to be a boxer, don't you?"

"Yeah!" That sounded like a great idea to Eugene. "I want

to be the best boxer ever."

"Well, let's weigh you, and we'll get started." Baldwin pointed to a scale in the corner. Eugene stepped on the scale and stood there while Baldwin slid the scale's weights back and forth. "One hundred twelve pounds. You'll do as a bantamweight."

Using money he earned at the amusement park and doing errands, Eugene was soon working out every weekday at the gym. He lifted weights, skipped rope, and boxed with anyone who would step into the ring with him. He never complained, no matter how beat up he was afterward. And he impressed the other boxers with his speed and power. As a result, they showed him different punches and footwork to outbox his opponents.

By the time Eugene turned 17, he had bulked up his body and moved up to the lightweight class. Now he thought he was ready for a real match. But first he had to convince Baldwin. After weeks of Eugene's persistent pleading for a pro match, Baldwin finally arranged a 10-round match for Eugene on Thursday, November 9, 1911. The Irish boxer Bill Welsh would be his opponent at Liverpool Stadium.

When the night arrived, the boxing lineup also included a welterweight black boxer from the United States—Aaron Lister Brown, known as "the Dixie Kid." The Kid was paired with Johnny Summers, an English boxer, for a 20-round bout before Eugene's fight. Brown was known for his lightning-fast reflexes. He liked to fight with his hands at his side and his chin stuck out, daring the other boxer to hit him.

The bell clanged for the second round of the Dixie Kid's match. The Kid and Summers jabbed and danced around each other until the Kid slugged Summers on the chin with a right uppercut, followed by a smashing left hook to his head. Summers wobbled, his legs buckled, and he crashed unconscious to the canvas. The crowd roared its approval. The referee held the Dixie Kid's arm up signaling a knockout victory in the second round.

Sooner than Eugene expected, it was his turn. Welsh and Eugene touched gloves and retreated to their corners.

The bell clanged. Round one.

Eugene and the Irish boxer emerged from their corners. They warily tested each other with jabs and the occasional punch. Eugene was determined to win and used every trick he had been taught.

The two fighters slugged each other round after round. When the bell clanged the end of the tenth round, both boxers were thoroughly pummeled and bloodied—but both were still standing. The judges added up their scores. The referee held up Eugene's arm. The crowd erupted in applause. Eugene had won his first pro fight.

The Dixie Kid had taken a seat in the audience and was watching Eugene's victory. Impressed with his style, speed, and the fact that he was still standing, Brown approached Eugene with an offer: "How'd you like to come with me to London so's I can train you?"

Eugene didn't hesitate. He knew it was his big chance. "Yessir, I'd sure like that." He held Dixie's hands between his boxing gloves and shook them. "But let me ask Mr. Baldwin if that's okay."

The next day, Eugene found himself in London living with the Dixie Kid, his wife, and their infant daughter. They lived in Mrs. Carter's Boarding House, along with boxers and entertainers from around the world. It wasn't long before Eugene was training with the Dixie Kid and earning money by doing errands and odd jobs for the other boxers.

Within a year or so, Brown was finding almost weekly matches for Eugene in boxing clubs around London. He also landed matches in the prestigious Blackfriars Ring—a club where Eugene's boxing reputation grew with each fight.

Eugene had never been happier, but France was still beckoning to him. He asked the Kid if he could arrange a match for him in Paris.

Months passed.

Then in October 1913, Brown approached Eugene while he was sparring. "I've arranged a 10-round match with Georges Forrest. It'll be in Paris on the 3rd of December."

Eugene unlaced his gloves and threw them high into the air.

"Yes!" Eugene shouted, dancing in the ring and jabbing at an imaginary opponent. "I'm going to France."

Eugene Bullard began boxing as a teenager and soon began competing internationally in places as far away as Egypt.

3

Paris

City of Lights

The weeks before the match passed slowly for Eugene, who could think of nothing but France. Finally, the departure day—pleasantly cool and sunny—came late in November. Eugene and Brown headed for the Victoria train station. After a few hours of enjoying the train ride and the passing scenery, they stepped off in Dover. The pair headed for the docks and boarded a steamer boat headed for France. Soon they would be in Calais, a small French seaport city only 25 miles across the English Channel.

Eugene found his way to the bow of the steamer, where he stayed for the whole journey across the Channel. He strained for the first glimpse of the land of his dreams. A thrill shot through him as the coastline swelled into view on the horizon. It was France!

After the steamer tied up at the Calais dock, Brown and Eugene made their way with the other passengers down the gangway. Eugene looked around. The longshoremen wore blue denims, striped shirts and black berets—and they gestured wildly and spoke in an unintelligible, wonderful language.

It was even better than Eugene had imagined, but the two

travelers had no time to dawdle. They hurried to the nearby train that would take them to Paris. After they disembarked at the Paris train station that evening, Eugene grabbed the Dixie Kid by his arm and dragged him across the platform.

Pointing at the irresistible lights of the city, Eugene said, "I don't fight for a few days. If I can see some of the sights, I promise I'll win."

True to his word, Eugene fought 20 rounds in the Elysées Montmarte arena and beat his opponent, Georges Forrestal, on points. The French audience thought Eugene was a sensation and applauded his boxing style.

After three more days of sightseeing and enjoying the cafés and the French people, it was time for the pair to return to London.

Back home, Eugene pestered Brown for another match in Paris. He had tasted life in France. He knew he couldn't be happy anywhere else. Efforts, though, for another match in Eugene's weight class were unsuccessful. Reliving his once-in-a-lifetime experience in Paris every night, Eugene tossed and turned, unable to sleep well. He had to get back to France.

One sleepless night the answer flashed through his mind. If he couldn't box in Paris, he would work at any job that would get him there. Maybe he could work as an entertainer. A troupe of black youngsters called "Freedman's Pickaninnies" lived in his boardinghouse. He knew they performed on tours around Europe—and they performed in France.

Freedman's Pickaninnies were well-known for their comedy routines in which they hit each other with slapsticks—flat boards nailed at one end that made a loud, slapping noise when someone was struck.

Eugene was a natural-born entertainer and soon went on tour with the Pickaninnies throughout Europe and Russia. After the troupe performed to audiences in Paris, Eugene stayed behind. He wasn't leaving. He was finally in France where he belonged.

By the spring of 1914, Eugene had landed several small jobs and had fought a few boxing matches, making enough money to enjoy his new life. He learned to speak French. And he liked France so much he even changed his middle name to Jacques, the French equivalent of James, his given middle name.

Life was good for Eugene. He hoped his new life would last forever.

4

French Foreign Legion

A Call to Arms

In 1914, Europe was simmering with old hatreds and scores to settle. The Continent was composed of many countries, some still ruled by emperors and kings. Some of the countries had battled each other in earlier wars. And most of the countries had complicated alliances with other countries, promising to protect each other in case of attack.

France had an alliance with Great Britain and Russia. Russia had another alliance with Serbia, a country bordering the Austro-Hungarian Empire. And the Austro-Hungarian Empire had an alliance with Germany. All it would take was a spark to ignite the flame of war, and most of Europe would be drawn into war.

On June 28, 1914, Austria's Archduke Franz Ferdinand and his wife visited Sarajevo, the capital of Bosnia-Herzegovina. He had just inspected his troops who were training in Bosnia. But assassins from neighboring Serbia were waiting for Ferdinand in the streets of Sarajevo. They wanted to free Bosnia from the Austro-Hungarian Empire and unite it with Serbia.

When the procession of cars carrying the archduke drove by, the assassins threw a bomb at his car. But the bomb bounced off and exploded under the car behind it. Incredibly, the assassins had another chance later that same day when Ferdinand decided to visit the man wounded by their bomb. Ferdinand's driver took a wrong turn, stopped their car and began to back up. One of the assassins, a 19-year-old Serbian named Gavrilo Princip, ran up to the car with a pistol and killed both Ferdinand and his wife.

The assassins were caught a few days later, and it was discovered that their weapons had come from the small country of Serbia. Austria demanded that Serbia control its terrorists. And it made other nearly impossible demands. Austria believed other countries would not come to Serbia's aid and declared war on Serbia on July 28, 1914.

Austria was dead wrong.

Russia prepared for battle by moving its troops to its western borders facing Austria-Hungary and Germany. France, an ally of Russia, moved its troops and weapons to its eastern border adjoining Germany. Responding to the moves made by Russia and France, Germany mobilized its troops a few hours later.

Germany demanded that neutral Belgium allow German troops to march through its country to invade France. Belgium refused. Germany then declared war on both Belgium and France. Great Britain was responsible for ensuring Belgian neutrality, so Great Britain declared war on Germany. Then Austria-Hungary declared war on Russia. What was to be known as the Great War—and later, as World War I—had begun.

The Belgian army was no match for the Germans, who swept through Belgium toward France, burning towns and killing people. Trains across Europe and ships from Great

Britain brought soldiers by the hundreds of thousands to the battle lines. After fierce fighting, the French and British armies stopped the German advance in early September near the Marne River, east of Paris.

EUGENE HAD BEEN ENJOYING a good life in Paris, working as a sparring partner and fighting an occasional boxing match. He hadn't paid much attention to recent events, but he soon noticed that most of his French friends were missing. They had left the gyms in Paris for the battlefields.

When Eugene started getting news early in the war about the deaths of his friends, reality hit him. After seeing notices in the Paris newspapers pleading for volunteers—even foreigners—to fight the Germans, he decided to join to fight alongside his friends.

France could not legally accept foreigners into its armed forces—except in its Foreign Legion. But enlistment was five years in the Legion, and most people thought the war would be over soon, probably before Christmas. The French minister of war devised a solution: foreign volunteers could enlist in special "Marching Regiments" of the Foreign Legion for the duration of the war.

Eugene showed up at the nearest Paris recruiting bureau on his nineteenth birthday to join the Foreign Legion. He knew he was in top shape, so he figured he could pass a physical exam even if it was a tough one. But it didn't take long for him to realize the physical was only a cursory exam. After a few pokes, prods and questions, it was obvious the French would accept almost anyone willing to join.

On October 9, 1914, Eugene Jacques Bullard—serial num-

ber 22717—was sworn in as a member of the French Foreign
Legion. He was now officially a man and a proud defender
of France who looked forward to fighting the Germans. But
he wished he had told his father where he was. Perhaps he
wouldn't be angry at him any longer for running away.

I wish my father could see me now, he thought.

FIRST TASTE OF COMBAT

Bullard's training started immediately at the Tourelles Barracks in Paris. He stood in line with other recruits from many
other countries and was handed his legionnaire uniform, coat,
shoes, and kepi—a round, flattop cap with a visor.

The Legion training was rigorous. The next morning—
and all the mornings thereafter—reveille was at 4 A.M. After
dressing and breakfast—which was just coffee—the recruits
were trained in marching with fully loaded packs. After their
big meal of soup, coffee, wine, and dessert at 11 A.M., they
practiced combat techniques for the rest of the day.

Bullard thought the training was getting tougher every day,
but he noticed he was being hardened into a real soldier. He
was thankful he was in good shape to begin with. The recruits
were then issued rifles, and they spent more time learning how
to shoot, charge with their bayonets, and perform first aid.

The French had lost so many men in the first few months
of combat they had to shorten the training of volunteers. As a
result, on November 28, only five weeks into training, Bullard
and 60 other men were sent north of Paris to the trenches on
the Somme front. Marching to the tune of "La Marseillaise,"
the Third Marching Regiment made its way through throngs
of cheering Parisians on its way to fight the hated Germans.

French Foreign Legion pilots and infantrymen, including Eugene Bullard, pose outside tent barracks in Paris.

As the regiment neared the Somme front in heavy rain, the volunteer soldiers heard the distant thunder of artillery. Finally, 17 days after they left Paris, they approached the frontline trenches. The ground shook from the continuous barrage of exploding shells.

Bullard thought they were entering the gates of hell. The acrid smell of gunpowder and the stench of death permeated the air. Bits of shrapnel and bodies of French soldiers littered the ground. But Bullard didn't have long to worry about it.

With bullets flying past—thwipp, thwipp, thwipp—his fellow soldiers crawled toward the trenches that would be their lifeline. Bullard dropped to the ground and followed, hoping to reach relative safety before he was struck by shrapnel or a bullet.

At long last, Bullard reached the edge of a trench.

"Quickly, *mon ami*," a voice said. "Before the next salvo."

Bullard dropped over the edge and landed in a muddy trench partly filled with water from the rain. Soldiers huddled shoulder-to-shoulder against the front wall stacked with sandbags.

"Welcome to your home away from home," a rain-soaked soldier said.

"*Merci*—"

A whistling shell exploded near the trench with an ear-shattering boom that shook the ground. Clods of muddy earth and pebbles pelted them.

Bullard was soon shooting back at the Germans. He kept a close eye on the enemy. Whenever enemy soldiers would charge the French trenches, he and his fellow legionnaires would shoot at them. Each side also watched for a chance to snipe at a soldier careless enough to raise his head above a trench.

Corpses littered the no-man's land between the lines, but neither side dared gather their dead for burial. Anyone foolish enough to try would certainly be killed.

Astonishingly, on Christmas Day 1914, an unofficial ceasefire occurred between the enlisted men on the warring sides, and season's greetings were exchanged. The German soldiers opposite Bullard called out and said they would allow the French to gather and bury their dead. The French replied that the Germans could do the same. That done, the two sides emerged from their trenches, sang carols, and exchanged small gifts. They even kicked a ball around in a game of soccer. After nightfall, quiet fell over the trenches.

But when senior officers behind the lines got wind of the informal truce, they were outraged. The next morning, a German captain grabbed one of his men's rifles and took aim across no-man's land. A solitary bang. A spray of blood. A French soldier toppled into a trench with a bullet hole in his head. A cascade of gunfire erupted from both sides.

Once more, Bullard experienced the horror of seeing his comrades-in-arms wounded or killed. He hated the Germans. By the end of April, four months after he arrived in the rat- and lice-infested trenches, he was battle-hardened, but still alive.

Was it just a matter of time before he was killed, too?

THE BATTLE OF ARTOIS

New volunteers were sent from Paris to relieve the battle-weary soldiers. Bullard and the other legionnaires were ordered to a rest area north of Arras. On April 25, 1915, Bullard boarded a boxcar with the rest of his company, grateful for a respite from the awful fighting. As the train clickety-clacked along the rails, he found himself wondering if another large attack was looming. But for the time being, he was going to take it easy and rest. He closed his eyes.

The train shuddered to a stop and shook Bullard awake. He was in a small village called Bethonsart. One look at the thousands of tents, artillery pieces, shells and soldiers from different countries convinced him he was right about an imminent large attack. He didn't have much time for contemplation, however. Officers were barking at the men to get off the train.

Bullard rested only a few days in Bethonsart. It wasn't

Eugene Bullard and troops in the American Expeditionary Forces gather for a photo. Bullard is wearing the French aviator's dress tunic with jodhpurs, part of the loose dress code of the French military.

long before he was ordered into the rear trenches at Artois. His days were busy hauling supplies, reinforcing the existing trenches, and using a pick and shovel to dig smaller, new ones for telephone wires.

One day, while digging in the red mud of Artois, he heard a droning noise from above. He spied a small airplane flying to the German-occupied territory just a few miles away. Bullard leaned on his shovel and watched the plane fly overhead. *Maybe I could do that.* He shook his head. *No chance*, he thought. He returned to his digging, wondering what it was like up there among the clouds.

Ahead of Bullard lay the isolated Artois Ridge, held by the Germans since the previous autumn. The small mountain was strategically important to both sides. Badly needed coal fields were behind the ridge, and French railroad tracks there had been commandeered by the Germans.

Beginning on May 4, the French unleashed a heavy bombardment of artillery fire for a planned attack on May 7. Nearly a thousand large cannons, field guns, and mortars pounded the German lines for days with hundreds of thousands of rounds.

It started to rain the night before the planned assault, and Bullard had trouble sleeping in his waterlogged trench. On May 7—the morning of the planned attack—the ongoing torrential rain turned the trenches into nothing but gutters of running water. The enemy lines were invisible behind the curtains of water, so the attack was postponed for another two days. Hunched in a second-line trench, Bullard was soaked to the skin and miserable. *Waiting is almost worse than the fighting*, he thought.

The sun appeared on May 9. French artillery had been bombarding the Germans since midnight. The rains had stopped, wisps of vapor rose from the battlefield, and the French soldiers were positioned. After cleaning their rifles, they attached their long bayonets for a charge on the Artois ridge. At 10 o'clock sharp, the French soldiers, hoping to regain the ridge, clambered out of the first-line trenches in front of Bullard and sprinted toward the German line.

From his vantage point, Bullard watched intently as the legionnaires charged toward the Germans. Shells exploded among the men, killing them randomly as they made their way forward. German machine guns barked with rat-tat-tats, their bullets slicing from side to side and mowing down rows of soldiers as if they were nothing but weeds. Bullard wondered if he'd have the same courage.

He didn't have long to think. Orders came to leave his second-line trench and move forward into the first-line trench. He left the relative safety of his own trench and ran as fast as he could and jumped in the next trench. The bottom was a muddy mess and littered with bodies of dead soldiers mixed with bloody straw. He hardly noticed the now familiar smell of death and gunpowder.

Immediately, the men were ordered up ladders and out of their trench. Bullets snapped through the air. Some of Bullard's comrades fell back dead as soon as they reached the tops of their ladders. German artillery shells burst everywhere, pounding the ground and spewing black geysers of earth and hot metal shrapnel.

Bullard found himself running toward the Germans, dodging the deadly machine gun fire the best he could. Shells whistled down. He had no time to think. Deafening explosions repeatedly knocked him down. Each time, he got up and ran toward the Germans, trying to avoid tripping over the many dead soldiers scattered on the field.

The French soldiers fought their way over the ridge and through the enemy lines in only a few hours, surprising the Germans with their speed. Some Germans could do nothing but surrender; others dropped their weapons and fled. By nightfall, Bullard and the legionnaires had advanced over six miles and taken the ridge.

Unfortunately, the French hadn't planned on the legionnaires advancing so quickly. The French reserve troops had been held too far behind the lines, and they couldn't reach the front in time to hold onto the newly won ground. The

Germans quickly recovered and sent in fresh troops to attack the legionnaires.

Without any reinforcements, the surviving legionnaires were forced to retreat under intense fire—back to almost where they had started hours earlier. Bullard was furious. Many of his friends had been killed. And for what? Fewer than half of the 4,000 legionnaires who fought that day were still alive. In Bullard's company, only 54 out of 250 survived.

Bullard was lucky. He was one of the 54.

ATTACKS NEVER END

The next day, German artillery continued to rain down around Bullard, but he hardly noticed the explosions. He sat in his muddy trench, still exhausted and ruminating about the disastrous events of the previous day.

New orders ran through his trench. He snapped to attention. Fresh regular soldiers were arriving. The remaining legionnaires were ordered to leave and head away from the lines.

On the evening of May 10, 1915, Bullard straggled with his fellow survivors toward the destroyed village of Mont-Saint-Eloi for some well-deserved rest. Upon arrival in the smoking ruins, the weary legionnaires dropped their heavy knapsacks and found sheltered spots wherever they could. Several soldiers shared cans of sardines and chunks of cheese. Bullard sat with his back against the remaining wall of a small house. He soon dozed off to the rumbling of distant artillery.

It seemed to Bullard that he had no sooner closed his eyes than a loud boom shook him awake. Waves of shells whistled down on the village, seeking the resting legionnaires. More explosions followed. Each salvo got a little closer. The enemy must have watched them enter the village.

Orders came down. The legionnaires must move out of range. Bullard and the men quickly gathered up their equipment. They marched to a village even farther away where the guns could not reach them, and they could recuperate for a few weeks.

All too soon, Bullard's rest period was over. In June, he was in a trench again, preparing for an assault against Hill 119—a heavily defended German entrenchment near Souchez. French artillery had bombarded the site for hours until there was no response from the enemy.

It was a hot day. The sickly sweet smell of decaying bodies drifted on the faint breeze. Bullard's throat felt dry.

"Up and over, men!" came the now-familiar order.

Bullard dashed for Hill 119, past rotting corpses turning blue and green and buzzing with swarms of flies. The ground was pockmarked from hundreds of shell explosions. Pieces of bodies and uniforms had been churned together in the soil. He ran past a severed arm sticking out of the ground. Its fingers pointed away from the German line. A warning? Bullard quickly dismissed that thought and continued sprinting forward. *I'm a legionnaire.*

French sappers arrived first and quickly cut through the coils of German barbed wire defending their trenches. Bullard made his way through the openings, barely noticing the dead French soldiers who were caught on the wire. He neared the first enemy trench.

Unknown to the French, the Germans had fortified their positions with concrete bomb-proof bunkers. The enemy had merely waited inside until the French shelling had stopped.

German heads popped up from their trench in front of Bullard. The enemy unleashed a fusillade of rifle and machine-gun fire. Somehow, Bullard made it to the edge of the first trench without getting shot. Lying low, he peered into the trench and fired his rifle at anything that moved.

His rifle jammed. Without hesitating, he dropped over the edge and landed on top of some dead soldiers in the bottom of the trench. Other legionnaires followed. Bullard had often wished he could fight the enemy with his bare hands. Now he found himself facing German soldiers man-to-man.

Bullard went wild. He threw away his rifle and pried another one from the hands of a dead German soldier. Using the rifle as a club and yelling "*Vive la France!*" and "*Vive la Légion!*," he bashed many enemy soldiers to death. Men who slipped and fell were trampled to death. The desperate hand-to-hand combat raged until the last German was killed.

Only a week later, Bullard found himelf in another major battle. Once more, the legionnaires marched into the front lines, while the Germans tried to move into French-held territory. Artillery bombardment rained down continuously. German machine gun fire was so intense, bodies rolled like leaves across no-man's land when they were struck by stray bullets. Bullard and his fellow legionnaires gathered corpses and stacked them like firewood for protection from incoming shells and bullets. But, in the end, Bullard and the remaining legionnaires successfully repelled the German assault.

After this battle, there were not enough legionnaires left alive in Bullard's Third Marching Regiment to fill its ranks. On July 13, Bullard and his comrades stood at attention in a ceremony that merged all the survivors into one regiment—the elite French Foreign Legion First Regiment. Bullard stood at attention, tall and proud. From now on he was no longer a member of a marching regiment. He was a full-fledged French legionnaire.

The colonel inspecting the troops stopped in front of Bullard and awarded him a promotion to corporal for his valor. He saluted; the colonel returned the salute and shook Bullard's hand.

For a brief moment, Bullard forgot the horrors of the battlefield.

The Battle of Champagne

After resting several weeks in the Vosges Mountains, Bullard rode north on a train to Chalons-sur-Marne. After a day's rest, Bullard and the legionnaires marched at night to the front lines at Suippes. The French lines, stretched 20 miles between the River Aisne and the Moronvilliers Hills, faced formidable German defenses.

The Germans had dug a labyrinthine web of trenches that stretched for miles. Machine guns were positioned everywhere. The Germans' underground shelters were fortified to withstand direct hits by artillery shells. Barbed wire was strung along their lines, facing the French.

Bullard and his fellow soldiers stood at attention while officers held up steel helmets. They explained the helmets were to protect the soldiers from head wounds. The soldiers were told to immediately discard their cloth kepis. Scattered grumbling traveled through the ranks. Bullard removed his kepi. He wasn't sure whether he liked the helmets, either, but he placed one on his head and fastened its straps.

Next, gas hoods were handed out to the troops in case the Germans used poison gas in the upcoming attack. Bullard tried one on. The clumsy canvas hood was hot and heavy and restricted his vision. He looked up. Through the hood's goggles, he saw another German airplane buzzing high in the sky, probably spying on what was happening on the French side. Bullard removed his gas hood. That was enough. He hoped he would never have to use it.

For three days, French artillery, large and small, pounded the German lines with millions of shells. Bullard recognized the sharp, metallic twang of the French 75s as they fired. Their shells whistled overhead and dug holes eight to ten feet across, destroying the enemy trenches. Bullard wondered how anyone could survive that bombardment, but the Germans continued firing back with their 77s and much larger cannons. Flashes of red fire, geysers of black smoke, and sprays of dirt erupted everywhere in the fields. Shrapnel shells exploded overhead, pieces of metal whizzed toward earth, shattering trees and rattling on the roofs of bunkers.

The morning of September 25, 1915, was cold and damp. The rain had turned the battlefield into boot-sucking mud. At 9:15 A.M., Bullard went over the top of his trench and slogged his way to the German line, dropping to the ground whenever he heard a shell coming his way. He kept moving forward, though, past the bodies of his fellow soldiers. Finally, that evening, the legionnaires captured the village of Souain-en-Champagne.

The legionnaires were then ordered to continue advancing to the town of Vouziers, about 25 miles to the west, to retake a strategically important piece of land named Navarin Farm;

its farmhouse had been destroyed by the Germans.

Bullard and his men reached the French lines near Vouziers by mid-afternoon on September 28. They moved through the trenches and the regular French troops, who were waiting for their orders. The legionnaires rushed toward Navarin Farm. But German machine gun and rifle fire, along with a rain of artillery shells, killed many of the legionnaires.

A flash. A deafening explosion.

Bullard lay stunned on the ground for a few moments. He tried to focus on the blood on his hand. He wiped it off and discovered his hand was not bleeding. His limbs seemed to move without any problems. He wiped his brow and winced. A small piece of metal had struck him in his forehead. He pulled it out. Blood from the cut flowed down his face and into his eyes.

Bullard removed his helmet and noticed several dents. Maybe the helmets were a good idea, after all. He grabbed a bandage from his first-aid kit, wound it around his head and replaced his helmet. *A legionnaire never quits.* He forced himself up and made his way closer to the Germans.

That evening, fresh legionnaire reinforcements arrived to help Bullard's company. But, by daybreak, they found themselves almost completely surrounded by enemy troops. The legionnaires knew that it was certain death for them unless they mounted a last-chance attack. Screaming like wild men, Bullard and the legionnaires charged the Germans. Once the Germans realized who they were facing—they knew legionnaires didn't take prisoners—they dropped their weapons and fled Navarin Farm.

Only a few legionnaires survived the awful battle, but

Navarin Farm was now in French hands. With so few of his comrades left, Bullard wondered what was going to happen to his company of soldiers.

AFTER THE BATTLE OF CHAMPAGNE

Five days after Bullard fought his way to the German lines in the Battle of Champagne where so many of his comrades were lost, fresh German reinforcements arrived. The Germans launched a counterattack and regained all the ground the French had taken. The battle was disastrous for the French. They had lost 145,000 men. All for nothing.

In a pouring rain, Bullard was ordered back to the reserve trenches behind the French lines. The trenches were nothing but muddy rivers, so the legionnaires found shelter in shell holes and under splintered trees and tried to stay as dry as they could.

Worse, though, were the thousands of bodies and body parts of fellow soldiers littering the fields and mixed into the mud. Bullard helped bury corpses in shallow graves. The men dug holes in the mud, rolled the bodies in and then furiously shoveled dirt over them. Sometimes, after the grave was filled in, rigor mortis caused an arm or leg to rise up through the loose dirt—a gruesome sight.

The commander gathered together the few surviving legionnaires. "Men, you have two choices," he said. "Either you go to Africa as legionnaires or you can transfer to a regular French regiment."

Bullard decided to transfer to the 170th Infantry Regiment because that regiment had fought alongside the legionnaires during the Battle of Champagne. He knew they were fierce fighters—so fierce that the Germans called the 170th the "Swallows of Death."

Shortly after transferring, Bullard changed from his khaki legionnaire uniform with the number "1" on the collar to a blue uniform with "170" on the collar. Not much else changed, though. Bullard found himself in a trench only a mile from where he had fought during the Battle of Champagne as a legionnaire.

After a successful battle to take the small village of Somme-py, Bullard was ordered to Belfort for an awards ceremony. He and his fellow 170th soldiers were awarded a *fourragere*, an ornamental braided cord worn over the left shoulder of a dress uniform.

For two months, Bullard rested in the village of Givry-en-Argonne, which gave him a needed respite from the horrors of war. On the morning of February 17, 1916, he was awakened by the rumble of military trucks. The soldiers were ordered to leave immediately.

Bullard packed his equipment and hopped into the back of a truck. For the next three days, the trucks bounced and ground their way along cratered roads to an unknown destination. Finally, on the morning of February 20, the trucks stopped. They could go no farther; German shells had completely cratered the roads. Hundreds of thousands of marching French troops and horse-drawn artillery streamed past them, all going in the same direction. The trucks unloaded their human cargo, and the soldiers continued on foot.

Bullard passed by a forlorn road sign pointing in the direction he was heading. All he could read was the word "Verdun."

THE BATTLE OF VERDUN

When Bullard finally arrived in Verdun on February 22, 1916, the weather was cold, damp and foggy. Unknown to him, the Germans had massed more than a thousand pieces of artillery near Verdun in an area only eight miles wide. The artillery pieces ranged from 77mm field guns to 380mm naval guns to the "Big Berthas," which fired shells that were as tall as a man and weighed a ton each.

The Germans stayed hidden in cleverly camouflaged underground concrete bunkers strong enough to withstand any French bombardment. German airplanes and huge Zeppelins swept the skies, searching for any French airplanes bold enough to spy on them. German troops had conquered Verdun before in 1792 and 1870—and now they lusted for another victory.

German artillery shells rained down in a cataclysmic continuous thunder until practically nothing was left alive. Soldiers were blown to pieces, their pieces blown into smaller pieces and churned into the roiling soil. The French were forced to retreat. But they did not surrender.

The next day, Bullard's unit was ordered to the village of Vaux near Verdun as a machine-gunner replacement for the 42nd and 44th infantry regiments, which were down to only a few men. As he marched through the shell-pocked desolation on his way toward Vaux, he shuddered at the horrible sights. Parts of bodies and ropes of entrails hung from broken trees like hideous Christmas ornaments.

The infantry regiments warmly greeted their replacements. The latest model gas masks, replacing the troops' hoods, were passed out. And the new men were shown how the trenches were reinforced with sandbags and logs to better withstand artillery shelling. For almost a week, Bullard's regiment fought and held its position despite German efforts to dislodge it.

On March 1, Bullard and the other machine-gunners were ordered to set up their weapons. All day long, waves of Germans advanced toward the French. And all day long, Bullard mowed them down—until the French artillery barrage took over that night.

The next day started with more German bombardment. This time there was a difference. Each shell burst with a dull thud, spraying a whitish mist that drifted toward the French soldiers.

"Poison gas!" someone shouted. "Put on your gas masks, immediately!"

A soldier to Bullard's right started coughing and fumbling with his mask. Bullard quickly grabbed his own gas mask and strapped it over his face before the poisonous cloud enveloped him. Bullard then went to the distressed soldier and helped him with his mask before he inhaled a lethal dose.

Commands came that afternoon to retreat about a half mile and await further orders. Bullard and his gun crew took shelter in the rubble of a shelled farmhouse.

Bullard covered himself with a mattress for protection. "And you do the same with whatever you can find," he ordered his men. Within seconds, a shell landed in a far part of the farmhouse and blew out a wall. Germans had seen them enter the house.

Before they could make a move, another shell burst through the roof above them and exploded with a blinding flash and a deafening boom. Something hard smashed into Bullard's mouth. It felt like someone had hit him with a shovel. The mattress had protected him—he was still alive—but a shard of shrapnel had sliced through and knocked out most of his teeth.

Dazed and bleeding profusely from his mouth, Bullard emerged from under his mattress. He administered first aid to his 11 wounded men. Four men didn't need aid, though—they were dead. One had been cut in half by the explosion.

Bullard had to tell his commanders about the condition of his men. He ran toward the command post, which was in a demolished house near the edge of Vaux. One after another, shells burst near him. He threw himself down whenever he heard a whistle coming too close. Once the shell had exploded, he got up and ran again. In the growing darkness, he spied the well-hidden entrance in the rubble.

Just as he reached the opening, Bullard heard a whistling noise grow louder and louder and suddenly fade away. *This one is going to get me!* He lunged toward the command post. A sudden explosion behind Bullard hurled him through the doorway.

Inside, Commander Nouvion and Captain Paleolouge sat at a table with a lighted candle, which was instantly blown out by the blast. Unseen, Bullard flew over their table and crash-landed in a dark corner.

"*Sacre bleu,*" Commander Nouvion said. "That was close."

"*Oui,*" Bullard said.

The officers jumped up. "Who's there?"

"Corporal Bullard, *mon Commandant.*"

"How did you get here?"

Bullard wiped the blood from his mouth. Gesturing, he explained how the explosion threw him inside and what had happened to his men. Captain Paleolouge grabbed a first-aid kit, and he and Bullard ran through the incoming shells back to the farmhouse. After the captain examined the casualties and dressed their wounds, he ordered Bullard to the rear lines for treatment.

"Non, mon capitaine," Bullard replied. "I must stay with my men."

That night, the still-bleeding Bullard gathered the un-injured men from his company to go with him behind the lines, east of Verdun.

Wounded Again

On March 3, 1916, after marching miles overnight, the totally exhausted and bloody Bullard arrived at the Chevert Barracks east of Verdun. Bullard and his men were so tired, they could hardly eat the hot food they were given without dozing off. With his mouth still hurting, Bullard gingerly finished some soup and found a clear spot in a corner. He dropped his knapsack to use as a pillow, then collapsed to the floor and promptly fell asleep.

Bullard had less than one day's rest. The next morning, word spread that unrelenting German artillery and thousands of German foot soldiers had forced the French 170th Infantry out of a village called Douaument. Bullard and his machine gun crew were ordered to retake the village. Carrying his machine gun and carbine, Bullard left that night and marched with his men until they reached the lines near Douaument.

As soon as the sun rose on March 5, an incredible German bombardment blasted huge craters in the no-man's land and the French lines. Untold numbers of machine gun bullets zipped through the air. Many bullets found their mark and killed unlucky French soldiers.

Bullard added to the melee by shooting belt after belt of machine gun ammunition at the advancing German troops. He stopped only when an enemy shell exploded nearby, raining him with stones and clods of earth. As new lines of gray-uniformed Germans headed his way, Bullard mowed them down with deadly accuracy.

Another shell exploded with a loud kaboom only a few feet away, showering him and his machine gun with more dirt. Steam hissed from the hot machine gun barrel. Bullard's ears rang from the concussion. He shook his head to clear his senses, and he brushed away the dirt on his gun. He tried firing. Nothing. He pulled the trigger again and again. Still nothing.

His smoking machine gun was too hot to operate. And it was jammed with all the dirt. Bullard fumbled with the gun, trying to get it working again, but failed. He had to get out of there. The Germans were still advancing.

Bullard kicked the mechanism of his machine gun, smashing it so the Germans wouldn't be able to salvage the weapon. He grabbed his carbine and hurried to the rear lines, diving in holes whenever he heard incoming artillery. Two shells screeched down near Bullard, who dove into the nearest deep crater, landing in soft dirt. He hunkered down and rolled over onto his back, breathing heavily.

Another soldier crawled over the edge of Bullard's hole. Bullard noted with a start that the soldier was wearing a gray uniform. A German! Bullard and the soldier locked eyes. Before the young German could react, Bullard pulled up his carbine and shot him twice in the chest. The soldier's last expression was one of surprise before he slumped into the bottom of the hole. Bullard scrambled out of his temporary shelter and raced to the safety of the rear lines, adrenaline pumping through his body.

As soon as night fell, Captain Paleolouge ordered Bullard and 13 other men to sneak through the lines and find another machine gun, ammunition, food and water. Somehow, the scavenging men located what they needed and headed back. As they passed through a small forest of broken trees, illumination-shells bursting overhead cast eerie shadows. Puddles of water reflected the violet flashes of artillery shells as they exploded on the French lines. The German attack was sure to come at dawn.

A blinding flash. A tremendous thump. Bullard awoke, dazed and lying on the ground. He had terrible pain in his left thigh. Exploring his leg with his hand, he found a large, bleeding gash. With bloody, slippery hands, he fumbled for the tube of iodine in his pack, broke off its tip and poured the contents into his wound. Even more intense pain immediately shot through Bullard's leg. He bit off a scream.

After the pain subsided to a dull, rhythmic pounding, Bullard worked his way to his feet using his carbine for support. Ten of his men had been killed or wounded by the shell that had punched a hole in Bullard's leg.

Bullard and the other survivors hobbled toward the village of Fleury for treatment by the medical corps and Red Cross. After examining Bullard, the Red Cross crammed him in an ambulance with seven other soldiers for transportation to Bar-le-Duc, an evacuation point for wounded soldiers. Even on his stretcher inside the ambulance, Bullard could feel every bump and hole on the rough road as the vehicle carefully worked its way through the night.

Another blinding flash. Another tremendous thump. The ambulance shook and lurched to a stop. A shell had exploded, blasting a huge crater in the road in front of them. They could go no farther. And there was nothing they could do. The exhausted and bleeding men lay there, lost in their thoughts; they eventually fell asleep.

Bullard awoke at daybreak and peeked outside. Nothing was moving. But none of the men dared leave the relative safety of the ambulance. Anything that was seen moving during daylight near the front lines would be an instant target.

The eight soldiers and the driver huddled inside the stalled ambulance for the entire day. They moaned and dozed, ate their rations and even used the vehicle to relieve themselves. Night finally came. Men repaired the road, and the ambulance once again started its slow journey. Late in the afternoon of March 7, the men arrived at Bar-le-Duc.

Bullard and hundreds of other wounded soldiers were loaded on stretchers, placed on a Red Cross train and shipped away from the lines to southern France. The train stopped at towns with hospitals along the way to unload some of the wounded and those who had died. By the next morning, Bullard could no longer hear the rumble of artillery.

On March 10, the Red Cross train pulled into Lyons, the third largest city in France and home of an important military hospital, the Hôtel Dieu. Bullard was cleaned up and put in a clean bed, and his wound was repaired by a surgeon.

Painful infections slowed the healing of Bullard's leg and kept him in the hospital for the next three months. While there, doctors also performed extensive dental surgery to repair his mouth. During those long months, he had plenty of time to think about the experiences he had just gone through.

Will I be able to fight again? Or do I even want to?

Healing and Medals

Bullard was transferred to a private clinic run by Madame Nesme less than a mile from his hospital. Madame Nesme, a member of a wealthy family, had volunteered to pay for the care of 32 soldiers. Bullard was one of the lucky ones she chose. The care at the Nesme clinic was excellent and, eventually, Bullard was able to hobble about with crutches.

One morning, Madame Nesme took Bullard aside. "Monsieur Bullard, I have learned that in 10 days you are to be awarded the Croix de Guerre for heroism." She took his hand. "Thank you for what you've done for France."

Bullard was speechless. He wondered what he had done that was so special. He finally stammered, "*Merci, madame.*"

During the next 10 days, Bullard practiced walking without crutches and was finally able to get around with a cane. The cane helped him stand at attention at the awards ceremony at the Place des Armes. A French general read a citation about Bullard's bravery in the Verdun battle and how he had helped his wounded comrades at a farmhouse there. The general pinned the prestigious Croix de Guerre medal on Bullard's tunic, stepped back and saluted him.

A crowd of wounded soldiers and grateful inhabitants of Lyons yelled, "*Bravo*, Bullard!" and "*Vive le 170th!*"

Bullard never felt so proud.

As time passed, Bullard's leg grew stronger, but doctors

Bullard, dressed in a French aviators' uniform, displays the medal he earned for valor at Verdun in 1916.

doubted that he'd ever walk without a limp. Bullard's daily exercise proved them wrong, though, and he finally discarded his cane. He enjoyed his life at the clinic and his new friends and acquaintances he met at parties there. Something, however, was bothering him. He didn't want to be a freeloader, but he had nowhere to go. And he missed his fellow French soldiers who were still fighting at the front.

During Bullard's stay at the clinic, many friends of the Nesme family visited the wounded men to cheer them up. Some were French military officers, such as Commandant Ferrolino, who was in charge of the French Flying Service at Brun.

One night, Ferrolino and Bullard were talking. "Eugene," the commandant said, leaning forward, "what do you want to do with your life once you're released from here?"

Bullard's feelings rose to the surface. Perhaps there was another way to fight for France. He remembered the airplanes flying overhead. "I'd like to be a gunner for the air service."

A look of surprise flashed across the commandant's face. Then he grinned. "*Trés bien!* When you are ready, Eugene, I will have you transferred to aviation."

Bullard grinned, too. Now he had something to look forward to.

5

Lafayette Flying Corps

A Bet

By mid-summer, Bullard was frequently given leave from the clinic so he could visit Paris. One afternoon, he stopped at a popular hangout for artists, La Rotonde, on Boulevard Montparnasse.

Two painter friends were already waiting for Bullard. Gilbert White, a successful American painter from Michigan, sat with Möise Kisling, a prosperous expatriate Polish painter in Paris. He had recently received a $5,000 inheritance from the first American pilot to die for France, Victor Chapman, who had been a mutual friend of Bullard and Kisling before his plane was shot down during a dogfight near Douaument. The two painters waved Bullard over to their sidewalk table.

Another American friend from Mississippi, Jeff Dickson, soon showed up and joined the group. The waiter brought a round of vermouth cassis drinks for everyone, and the four men engaged in lively discussion about art and the war.

"What are you going to do when you get out of the hospital?" Dickson asked Bullard.

"I'm planning on going into the air service."

Dickson snorted. "No way."

Kisling set his drink down. "What exactly do you mean by that crack?"

"You know what I mean," Dickson answered. "Eugene's colored. There are no Negroes in the air force. There's no way he'll ever become an aviator in France or anywhere else."

Kisling raised his voice. "If Eugene says he can become an aviator, I believe him."

Dickson turned to Bullard. "I'll bet a thousand dollars you can't." He paused. "No, make it $2,000."

"You know that I don't have that kind of money," Bullard said. "But I will become a flyer."

When Dickson excused himself to use the restroom, White turned to Bullard. "Eugene, if you say you can do something, Möise and I know you can. We'll cover your bet."

The next day, the foursome met once more at La Rotonde. Bullard pulled out $2,000 given to him by his friends and laid it in front of Dickson. "I'm taking you up on your bet. The next time you see me, I'll be an aviator."

Dickson blanched. "Okay, okay. I figure it's a pretty safe bet, anyway. No colored guy is going to fly."

"I'll hold the money," White said.

Everyone clinked their glasses together, agreeing to the terms of the bet.

Bullard was now on a mission. The next day at the clinic, he found Commandant Ferrolino. Bullard announced that he was ready to leave for the aviation corps.

The commandant kept his earlier promise and contacted officials in the French Air Service on Bullard's behalf. A week or so later, Bullard opened a telegram. He could hardly believe his eyes. He had to read the message again. And again. It was

A French Air Service ID photo taken early in Eugene Bullard's air training. On the left, he's wearing an insignia of the French Air Service; on the right is his Croix de Guerre awarded for valor at Verdun.

true. He was ordered to report to Caz-au-lac on October 6, 1916, for training as an aircraft machine gunner.

Bullard could hardly wait.

Penguins and Other Planes

The morning of October 7 arrived. Bullard, sound asleep in one of the barracks at Caz-au-lac, was suddenly awakened by reveille. Eager to begin aviation machine-gun training, he leapt out of his bed, cleaned up and joined the other men forming outside. He recognized Edmond Genet, one of his fellow soldiers from the Foreign Legion.

"Edmond," Bullard said, shaking his friend's hand. "What's a legionnaire doing here?"

"I'm now a pilot in the Lafayette Escadrille," Genet replied. "And I'm here to learn how to shoot a machine gun, because I fly a one-seater aircraft, a Nieuport. I have to do everything myself—fly the plane and shoot at the same time."

"The Lafayette Escadrille?"

"Yeah, it's an American volunteer squadron."

"And you're a pilot?"

Genet smiled. "It beats the trenches. And I get paid more than an aviation machine gunner—$10 more a month."

Bullard thought for a moment. "I never heard of the Lafayette Escadrille, but for $30 a month, I'd just as soon be a pilot, too."

The next day, Bullard visited his captain and announced that he'd rather become a pilot. The captain promised he would forward Bullard's request to his superiors.

While waiting for his request to be answered, Bullard practiced for the next two weeks, shooting machine guns at

The Blériot Penguin flightless monoplane with clipped wings and a low-power three-cylinder engine was used to train pilots in engine control and ground handling.

moving targets while trundling along a track in a mockup of a cockpit. He fired at targets from motorboats. And to determine the accuracy of his shooting, he even fired at real planes flying overhead, using guns that shot photos—not bullets—whenever he squeezed the trigger.

Bullard's orders to become a pilot finally came, and he started his pilot training at an aviation school in the city of Tours. His first assignment was to learn how to handle a Blériot monoplane on the ground. The Blériot had a three-cylinder 45-horsepower rotary engine and wings only about five feet long. The pilots called them "Penguins" because they couldn't fly.

A group of veteran pilots and Penguin graduates gathered near the airfield and joked as the Penguins were brought from the hangars. Bullard realized that they wanted to watch the new trainees in their Penguins. And he also noticed their faces—all smiles.

After crawling into the cockpit, Bullard buckled in and fastened his helmet. One of the French instruction monitors showed Bullard the Penguin's simple controls: rudder pedals, a joystick, and an ignition cut-off switch.

Bullard was instructed to taxi the Penguin in a straight line. "Give the machine full gas," the monitor instructed. "Get the tail off the ground at once. Use your rudder pedals to keep it going straight."

A mechanic yelled, "Switch off."

Bullard made sure his ignition switch was off. "Switch off."

The mechanic flipped the propeller over a couple of times to suck in gas.

Bullard snapped the ignition switch on. "Contact."

The mechanic yanked the propeller down as hard as he could. The engine coughed and roared to life. Bullard pulled back on the gas control for full gas.

Okay, Bullard thought, *how hard can this be?* His Penguin picked up speed, lifted its tail and zig-zagged down the airfield at 50 miles per hour. Almost immediately, he found himself swerving to the right. He pressed his foot too hard on the left rudder pedal. Then he found himself swerving to the left. He pressed on the right pedal. Without warning, he started whirling in circles as if the plane was chasing its own tail. Each time Bullard completed a circle, he could see the pilots near the hangars waving their arms and laughing.

Bullard wasn't the only student pilot having problems. The other Penguin pilots were darting about and spinning in circles. One Penguin tipped over on its nose, leaving the student pilot hanging upside down in its cockpit. By late morning, gusty winds stopped the practice. A bit embarrassed, Bullard crawled out of his cockpit to laughter and good-natured ribbing from the spectators.

After a few days, Bullard mastered his straight-line taxiing technique and graduated into phase two, the rolling class.

The second part of his instruction was flying another Blériot called a Roleur. It had full-length wings and could fly, but Bullard was strictly instructed not to lift off the ground. He had to taxi back and forth on the field to get the feel of the controls, and he had to practice for three straight weeks until he got it right.

Finally, the day came when Bullard was allowed to fly. Using the same Roleur, he was instructed to lift off the ground about three feet and fly a short distance. Then he had to shut off the engine and land the plane. He repeated that exercise over and over until his instructor said he could fly at 500 feet, but in a straight line. The only turn allowed was the one when he had to return to the airfield.

Bullard roared down the field and felt the air lift the plane. He pulled back on the joystick and kept climbing until he leveled off at 500 feet. Only then did he dare a glance at the fields and trees passing below him. I'm a real pilot now, he thought. The engine droned on. He smelled the haze of castor-oil-based engine oil and felt the cold wind against his face. He was too busy to do more than glance at the countryside below him. All too soon, he had to turn and head for home.

He swung his joystick to the left and pressed his rudder pedal. His Blériot turned left and pitched upward a bit before Bullard compensated. By now, he also knew that if he had turned right, the plane had a tendency to pitch downward—a result of its rotary engine torque.

Before the day of his final test, he had to perform a series of aerial maneuvers at 2,000 feet, shut off the engine and then glide with power off to a predetermined landing spot. Graduation day arrived. Bullard was a little nervous, particularly with all the instructions coming at him from his monitor: *do this, don't do this, and when you come back, fly over the field twice, push on the joystick to come down, and cut the engine before you land.*

Bullard did what he was told and headed back for the airfield. He circled it twice and realized he was confused. Did you push the joystick first and then cut the engine or was it the other way around? He circled the field again. So many instructions were swirling in his head, they were nothing but a muddled mess. He couldn't make up his mind what to do. He circled again. For almost an hour he circled the field until he ran out of fuel.

Well, at least that solved my problem, he thought. He glided to a landing, bounced a few times on the grass field, and came to a stop.

His flight instructor and aircrew ran across the field to greet Bullard as he clambered out of the cockpit.

"Congratulations," the instructor said, shaking Bullard's hand. "I don't know why you kept circling the field, but you passed the test."

Bullard's knees felt weak. He had made it.

On May 5, 1917, Eugene Bullard was awarded military pilot certificate #6950. He was now a pilot. After wings were pinned to his uniform, he was given a six-day leave in Paris.

Perfect, Bullard thought. *I have some unfinished business there.*

SETTLING A BET

Bullard arrived in Paris with his pilot's certificate in his pocket and knocked on Möise Kisling's studio door.

"Why, it's Eugene!" Kisling exclaimed. "What are you doing here?"

With a smile, Bullard reached into his pocket, took out his pilot's certificate and unfolded it in front of his friend's face.

"Why, you old devil . . ." Kisling grabbed Bullard's hand and vigorously shook it. "Congratulations. Come in. I must tell Gilbert."

Bullard found a chair and sat down while Kisling phoned Gilbert White.

"Hello, Gilbert," Kisling said loudly. "Guess who's in town and guess who's got his pilot's certificate."

Bullard strained to hear the rest of the conversation, which went on animatedly for some time. He knew something was up.

Kisling finally hung up. "Eugene, we're going to Henri's Bar tomorrow for lunch with Gilbert. Gilbert also invited Jeff Dickson, who bet against you. He doesn't know you're in town." Kisling rubbed his hands together gleefully. "This is going to be fun."

The next day, Kisling and Bullard met White at Henri's a little early, and the three found a table before Dickson showed up. Bullard was resplendent in tan boots laced up to his knees and wearing a blue pilot's uniform with large, aviator wings sewn on his collar.

White drummed his fingers on the table while the trio waited for Dickson. Finally, a silhouette appeared in the bar's front door and strode toward them.

"Hello—" Dickson said. He gasped when he saw Bullard and his uniform. After his initial shock, he managed to say, "Well, I'll be. How in the world did you do it, Eugene?"

"I asked the French government to give me a chance, and here I am," replied Bullard.

"Well, I've obviously lost the bet." Dickson stuck out his hand to Bullard. "I hate to lose that kind of money, but I'm glad the first colored military pilot is you."

Bullard was suddenly rich—$2,000 rich—for the first time in his life. "Thanks. For once, let me pay for our lunch. And let's celebrate today. It's on me."

The foursome made the rounds of bars up and down the nearby streets, celebrating Bullard's achievement. By midnight, it seemed that most of Paris knew that a black American had become a military pilot.

During his six-day leave, Bullard got up the courage to write to his father for the first time since he left home more than 10 years earlier. In his letter, Bullard asked for forgiveness for running away. He said he thought of his father daily. He described his life in boxing, how he won many medals fighting in the French Foreign Legion, and how he was now the first black military pilot in the world.

Weeks later, Bullard received a reply from his father, who said he regarded Bullard as his number one son and that he had forgiven him for running away.

Bullard read the letter over and over. Finally, he put it back in its envelope and smiled. *My father's proud of me. I wish he could see me now.*

ADVANCED TRAINING

Even though Bullard had earned his wings, he was still not qualified for combat flying. To hone his skills, he was transferred to an advanced flying school at Châteauroux, where he learned to fly some of the most advanced planes available.

First, Bullard mastered the French Caudron G-3 biplane, with its twin tailbooms and open framework fuselage. Originally flown as an observation aircraft, it was a tough and reliable little plane. But its single 80-horsepower rotary engine gave it a lackluster performance of only 68 miles per hour maximum speed. Built from wood, canvas and wire, the fragile-looking planes were jokingly called "chicken coops" by the pilots.

A Caudron, one of the many planes Bullard flew.

Because G-3s were usually unarmed and vulnerable near the front lines, they were retired from combat in 1916 and then used as trainers by the French.

Next, Bullard stepped up to training in the Caudron G-4, a French biplane with twin 80-horsepower engines giving it a maximum speed of 77 miles per hour. The G-4 was derived from the G-3, but had longer wings, an additional seat for an observer-gunner in the front and four rudders instead of two. Armed with one machine gun and carrying up to 250 pounds of bombs, G-4s were flown by the French on reconnaissance or bombing missions over Germany.

Bullard had to work hard for his G-4 certification. He discovered that having two engines meant more than twice the work and skill level to fly it. But eventually he more or less mastered flying the larger plane. It was obvious, though, that Bullard was meant to fly the smaller, single-engine fighter planes.

At the end of June, Bullard transferred to the Avord School of Military Aviation for his final training before combat. One of the largest aviation schools in France, the Avord School had a three-mile long and half-mile wide grass airstrip with clusters of hangars that held hundreds of planes. A number of wooden barracks with red tile roofs accommodated offices, mess halls, and sleeping quarters for the pilots and instructors.

Bullard's flight instructors informed him that his duties would involve driving away enemy planes and escorting bombers and reconnaissance planes. He would also patrol the skies, looking for enemy aircraft to engage in combat.

Flying the latest types of planes, Bullard had to practice the intricacies of what he called "fancy flying." His aerobatic

The gates to the Avord School of Aviation, one of the largest in France, where Bullard learned how to fly.

instructors showed him how to execute changes of direction, perform rolls and corkscrews and how to attack out of the sun to prevent being seen by the enemy. He learned power dives for attacking from above or escaping attack from behind and how to pull up safely before he hit the ground. These were all necessary maneuvers for air combat, and they were maneuvers that might save his life one day.

Early combat planes had machine guns mounted on the top wing, so the bullets wouldn't hit the propeller. Wing-mounted guns meant the pilots had to reach up to fire them—not an easy task when flying violent maneuvers during air combat and trying to aim at enemy aircraft. But Bullard practiced firing the newest synchronized machine guns that could fire through the plane's whirling propeller blades without hitting them. Finally, he learned how to fly and fight in formation.

One day, on the ground, Bullard watched in horror as a plane buzzing overhead went into a dive and then struggled to pull up. As the plane neared the ground, its engine noise got louder and louder, and it was obvious that the plane was going to smash into one of the airfield buildings.

The plane crashed through the metal roof of the camp's bakery with a loud bang. A white cloud rose into the air. Luckily, no fire erupted. Bullard and a crowd of other pilots ran toward the bakery, expecting the worst. White-shirted bakers ran outside, cursing loudly.

As Bullard arrived at the crash, a flour-covered pilot crawled out of the crumpled wreckage and climbed down to the ground, apparently uninjured. A stunned crowd gathered around the pilot, who was covered from head-to-toe in white flour. Captain Boucher arrived and demanded to know what had happened.

The hapless pilot stepped forward, stood at attention and snapped a salute, a puff of flour wafting from his sleeve. "It was I, *mon capitaine.*"

The crowd erupted in laughter. The captain shook his head in disbelief. It wasn't the first time this pilot had crashed. But now there would also be a bread shortage for a while.

Bullard knew he was supposed to receive additional combat flying training, but instead he was placed in charge of his sleeping quarters at Avord. *What a strange order*, Bullard thought. But he felt it wouldn't be long before he was sent to the front.

His sleeping quarters were shared by 22 other American

pilots who had also volunteered to fly for the French. Bullard had gotten friendly with all the pilots—especially a tall American named Reginald Sinclaire, who slept only inches away in the next bunk. Bullard appointed Sinclaire his assistant and, together, they kept the American quarters spotless. The inspecting lieutenant announced they had the best-looking room in the barrack.

Eventually, Bullard started noticing that pilots who had arrived after him were shipped off to the front for combat. He was ready, too. And he was itching to go. What was the holdup? Rumors started trickling back to Bullard that an influential American in Paris disapproved of having a black pilot in the flying corps. After several weeks of being left behind by many of his comrades, Bullard started putting two and two together.

Bullard knew that Dr. Edmund Gros, an American doctor and commissioned major in Paris, had been instrumental in forming the Lafayette Escadrille. Dr. Gros was also the vice-president of a committee that oversaw the affairs of all the American pilots flying for France. Once a month, Dr. Gros would dole out 50 francs—donated by wealthy Americans—to every American pilot. But Bullard wasn't even aware of the arrangement until another pilot happened to mention it to him.

From then on, Bullard showed up every month at Dr. Gros's townhouse in Paris on the Avenue du Bois de Boulogne to receive his check. And every month, no matter how early he showed up, Bullard would be the last pilot to collect his check—withheld until the banks had closed and he couldn't cash it.

Bullard's pilot friend, Edmond Genet, finally took him

Dr. Edmund Gros, an American doctor and commissioned major living in Paris, was instrumental in forming the Lafayette Escadrille. He also made life difficult for Bullard.

aside and convinced him that someone really was working against him. Bullard then approached his commanding officer: "Captain Boucher, I wish permission to write to Colonel Girard."

Captain Boucher looked annoyed. "For what reason, corporal?"

"I want to ask why I'm being kept at Avord while France needs pilots at the front."

"Permission denied." Captain Boucher waved his hand. "You're dismissed."

Bullard simmered. It was August 5, 1917—almost three months after he received his flying diploma—and he still hadn't been sent to fight the Germans. *No doubt it was because of Dr. Gros. Now what?*

Three days later, however, Bullard received orders to report to Le Plessis Belleville, a combat flight school and final stop before being sent to the front. He couldn't believe it. Someone else must have heard of his plight and informed the right people.

His fellow pilots hoisted Bullard on their shoulders, danced, sang, and celebrated the good news. Over drinks at the canteen, some of the partying pilots let it slip that a certain American in Paris had done everything he could to keep Bullard from becoming a pilot because of his color.

Bullard knew they were referring to Dr. Gros, but he didn't care about that anymore. He had won. Now he was going to fight in the air for his adopted country—France—and nobody was going to stop him.

LAST STOP BEFORE AIR COMBAT

Bullard arrived at Le Plessis Belleville a few days later, ready to be assigned to a combat fighter squadron. The next day, after practicing maneuvers in a French Nieuport, he landed and was ordered to report to Captain Chevillard.

Bullard entered the captain's office and saluted.

"At ease, corporal." The captain shuffled some papers. "Your orders for deployment have been received from General Headquarters. But you have a six-day leave coming up, and I cannot tell you the details until you return."

Six whole days in Paris!

Whenever Bullard was in Paris, he discovered that he never had to pay for meals or drinks. The local citizens believed it was their duty to treat soldiers headed for the front. After looking up some old friends, he met a Parisian girl with a most unusual pet—a rhesus monkey. Bullard fondly remembered working with a capuchin monkey. The girl needed money, so Bullard convinced her to sell the monkey to him. Other pilots had mascots, such as dogs and even lion cubs. *Why not a monkey?* Bullard handed over a few francs and immediately had a small brown monkey sitting on his shoulder.

"I'm going to call him Jimmy," Bullard said to the girl. "Wait till my flying buddies see him."

Bullard was right. Upon his return to Le Plessis, the other pilots greeted Bullard and Jimmy with whoops of delight. Jimmy held on tightly to Bullard and chattered back with wide eyes at the pilots. But Jimmy soon felt comfortable with all the excitement swirling around him. From that day on, Bullard carried Jimmy in his flight jacket for good luck.

Tacked up on the bulletin board was a list of new assign-

Bullard was not the only one flying high in the sky. Jimmy, his pet monkey, often accompanied him on flights.

ments. Bullard ran his finger down the list and gasped. He had been assigned to Squadron Spa-93, one of the top escadrilles that flew French-built SPADs, some of the best fighter biplanes in the war. He bubbled with pride and hoped he could live up to the escadrille's famous reputation.

Bullard arrived at Spa-93's landing strips near the village of Beau-Zie-sur-Aire, not far from Verdun. He spent a week meeting his two new mechanics and practicing landings and aerial combat maneuvers in a SPAD VII.

The rugged SPAD was fast. Its Hispano-Suiza 150-horse-power inline engine gave it a top speed of 120 miles per hour during level flight. During a dive it could go as fast as 250 miles per hour. Equipped with a Vickers .303 caliber synchronized machine gun that fired through the propeller, it was a deadly fighting machine. But it was also dangerous for pilots who didn't learn its idiosyncrasies. The SPAD didn't glide well. And it was difficult to maneuver at low speeds. Even more dangerously, its thin wings gave it a very sharp stall without much warning at slow speeds. As a consequence, it was a difficult plane to land safely and not crash.

At the end of the first week in September, 1917, Commandant Ménard called Bullard into his office. "Corporal Eugene Bullard, do you consider yourself ready for combat?"

Bullard knew he was. "Yes, sir, I am quite ready."

"Very good," the reply came. "Your flight schedule is posted. You are going up tomorrow on a patrol. Don't get out of formation to do battle until you have a few hours of experience under your belt." The commandant smiled at Bullard. "We don't want Jimmy to become an orphan."

Before turning in for the night, Bullard placed Jimmy in a

wooden cage and covered it with a sheet. Then he headed for the mess hall and read the orders for the next day. He was one of 14 pilots scheduled to fly from 8–10 A.M. and from 4–6 P.M.

Bullard was ready. He just hoped he could sleep that night.

FIRST COMBAT FLIGHT

It was still dark when Bullard woke to the sound of a blaring horn calling the morning assembly. He quickly got into his fur-lined flying gear, laced up his boots, and picked up the chattering Jimmy from his cage. After grabbing his flying helmet and his customary French breakfast—a large cup of coffee—he stepped into the cold, predawn blackness and headed toward the flight line with Jimmy on his shoulder.

Except for an occasional artillery shell exploding miles away, the morning was quiet. As he got closer to the flight line, he could hear the soft footsteps of the other pilots approaching.

Bullard felt real fear. Soon, he would be climbing into his airplane and flying over the front. *The eyes of the world are watching me*, he thought. *I have to do or die, and I don't want to die.*

The SPADs were lined up wingtip-to-wingtip in two straight rows outside the hangars. A few minutes later, all the members of the patrol were gathered together near their assigned planes waiting for instructions.

Commander Ménard spoke up. "Rendevous with Captain Pisard at 6,000 feet. And take good care of Bullard. We don't want Jimmy left without a father."

All the men laughed, including Bullard.

"Now, up into the air, men," the commander ordered. "Quickly."

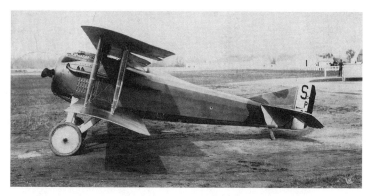

The SPAD S.VII was one of a series of biplane fighter biplanes produced by the Société Pour L'Aviation et ses Dérivées (SPAD). The sturdy fighter was known for its good climbing and diving performance.

Crew: 1
Length: 19 ft 11 in
Wingspan: 25 ft 8 in
Height: 7 ft 2 in
Empty weight: 1,124 lb
Max takeoff weight: 1,632 lb
Engine: Hispano-Suiza Aa V-8, 150 hp
Max speed: 119 mph
Service ceiling: 17,500 ft
Guns: 1 x .303-cal Vickers machine guns

The SPAD S.XIII, a highly capable French biplane fighter developed by the Société Pour L'Aviation et ses Dérivées (SPAD), was derived from the earlier model SPAD S.VII. The S.XIII had larger wings and rudder than the S.VII, a more powerful clockwise-rotation engine and an additional machine gun. The sturdy fighter was renowned for its diving speed. Due to thin wings, it glided poorly, and it had a very sharp stall, which made it difficult to land. Before WWI ended, 8,472 planes were manufactured.

Crew: 1
Length: 20 ft 6 in
Wingspan: 27 ft 1 in
Height: 8 ft 6.5 in
Empty weight: 1,245 lb
Max takeoff weight: 1,888 lb
Engine: Hispano-Suiza 8Be V-8, 220 hp
Max speed: 135 mph
Service ceiling: 21,815 ft
Guns: 2 x .303-cal Vickers machine guns

Each pilot dashed for his plane. Bullard climbed into his cockpit and fastened his helmet. Jimmy jumped to the floor and tugged on Bullard's pants—a signal that he was ready to climb inside Bullard's fur-lined jacket.

"Okay, Jimmy," Bullard said, picking him up. "In you go."

One of Bullard's mechanics yelled, "Switch off!"

"Switch off," Bullard replied.

The mechanic slowly turned over the propeller and stood back. "Contact!"

"Contact."

The mechanic reached up and quickly flipped the propeller blade toward the ground. Puffs of smoke shot out the SPAD's exhaust pipes. The engine sputtered to life. Bullard let it warm up while he checked his machine gun. A mechanic hopped on the lower wing and wiped the windshield and fastened Bullard's seatbelt; another held a rope ready to jerk out wooden chocks holding back the plane.

A signal. A salute from Bullard. The chocks were snatched away and his SPAD trundled to the airstrip. He gave it full throttle and raced down the field into the wind, the eager plane lifting off almost immediately.

Bullard climbed to 6,000 feet, leveled off and quickly found his place in the V-formation of 14 SPADs and Nieuports. Captain Pisard's plane led the way at the point of the "V." Six planes each—only a few feet apart—formed both legs of the "V," and one trailed behind, in the middle of the formation. For the first half hour, they flew back and forth on the French side of the line, always keeping a sharp lookout for the enemy.

In the hazy distance, Bullard could make out observation balloons floating above both sides. Farther still, Bullard saw a few circling enemy planes miles behind the German lines.

Keeping one eye on Captain Pisard for any signals, Bullard constantly swiveled his head—looking up, looking down, looking everywhere—for German aircraft. He wished he had another set of eyes.

Captain Pisard motioned for the formation to follow. He banked his plane and headed across the lines. *This is the real thing*, Bullard thought, with a sudden thrill. The formation dutifully followed behind its leader. Occasionally, Bullard would see bursts of ugly, gray smoke appear nearby in the sky. These were explosions from anti-aircraft artillery firing at them—what the British nicknamed "Archie." Luckily, Archie did not do any damage.

After flying miles into German territory to the city of Metz, the captain signaled for his men to return to the French side. Bullard looked down as he flew over Verdun. He saw the trenches and the fighting still raging below. He remembered

Anti-aircraft guns tried to shoot planes from the sky.

standing in those same muddy trenches and looking up at the airplanes flying overhead. Now, he was the pilot flying over the foot soldiers.

Without warning, the captain's plane suddenly banked to one side. The other planes instantly fell out of formation and scattered across the sky. Bullard's heart skipped a beat. *It's an attack!* He instinctively slipped out of formation, not wanting to be a target. He looked about wildly, his heart pounding, but he couldn't see any German planes. *Where are they?*

After a minute or so of everyone flying battle maneuvers, the captain flew past Bullard. The captain signaled for the pilots to form up again and fly back to home base. Bullard felt his arms quivering from the excitement. *What in the world was that all about?*

Bullard landed safely and taxied to his tie-down spot. After climbing out of his cockpit, Bullard was surrounded by the other pilots who slapped him on his back and stuck out their hands to congratulate him. There were no enemy planes. There was no air battle. It was only an initiation rite they always performed for the benefit of any new pilot. Everyone laughed. Bullard laughed, too. He was one of them now.

"Go take a rest," the pilots advised Bullard. "You have to fly again at four o'clock." Bullard felt revved up and not particularly tired. But after the 11 o'clock meal, he headed for his bunk and stretched out, still wearing his flying suit.

Sleep came instantly.

BLOODED
September 1917. Bullard awoke with a start.

The duty sergeant was still shaking his shoulder. "It's 3:30.

Time to get up, Bullard."

Bullard swung his body upright and rubbed his eyes. He stood up and stretched with an enormous yawn. He grabbed his helmet and let Jimmy out of his cage. The monkey clambered up on Bullard's shoulder and held on while Bullard headed toward the flight line.

Commander Victor Ménard stood next to his SPAD, waiting while the pilots approached. After the commander's men were gathered, he joked about Bullard's monkey. "Bullard, do you think your son will protect us today?"

The pilots laughed. Bullard's tension lessened a bit.

After a few minutes, the French SPADs and Nieuports had formed the now-familiar V-formation and were climbing through the cool air to 6,000 feet. Ménard signaled them to head for the front in the Verdun sector, a particularly dangerous area.

It wasn't long before Bullard spied a number of moving dots in the far distance. As the dots grew larger, it became obvious the dots were four large German bombers surrounded by 16 German fighter planes—Fokker triplanes—headed in the direction of Bar-le-Duc.

Ménard signaled for his fighters to prepare for combat and divide into two formations of seven planes each.

In an instant, the German triplanes dove toward the French. Planes flashed by Bullard in a kaleidoscopic whirl of aerobatics, punctuated by rat-tat-tats and the whiz of bullets whipping past. Bullard yanked his joystick about, maneuvering to avoid the attackers. He glimpsed smoke trailing from one bomber—then from two German fighters, each plunging to earth.

The Fokker Dr. I Dreidecker was a German triplane fighter produced by Fokker-Flugzeugwerke. The plane was slower than Allied fighters in level flight and diving, but it maneuvered well. It was the aircraft of choice for the famous German pilot, Manfred von Richtofen, who scored 80 victories before being killed.

Crew: 1
Length: 18 ft 11 in
Wingspan: 23 ft 7 in
Height: 9 ft 8 in
Empty weight: 895 lb
Loaded weight: 1,292 lb
Engine: Oberursel Ur. II 9-cyl rotary, 110 hp
Max speed: 115 mph
Service ceiling: 20,000 ft
Guns: 2 x 7.92 mm Spandau LMG 08/15 machine guns

One of the most successful French fighter planes of WWI, the nimble Nieuport Nie 17 was produced by the Société Anonyme des Etablissements Nieuport. The first planes were equipped with an over-the-wing Lewis machine gun, but the later models had a synchronized through-the-propeller Vickers .303 machine gun.

Crew: 1
Length: 18 ft 10 in
Wingspan: 26 ft 11 ins
Max takeoff weight: 1,246 lb
Engine: Le Rhône 9J 9-cyl rotary, 110 hp
Max speed: 110 mph
Service ceiling: 17,388 ft
Guns: 1 x .303-cal Lewis or 1 x .303 cal Vickers machine gun

Bullard maneuvered behind one Fokker that was desperately trying to shake Bullard's sky-blue SPAD. Bullard kept on his tail and managed to fire several bursts. Before Bullard could tell if he had even hit the plane, a stream of bullets slashed through the air over his cockpit.

Bullard whipped his plane into a twisting dive, then rose up to shoot at another plane that appeared in front of him. Bullard's heart pounded in rhythm with the rattle of his machine gun as it fired. The enemy plane jerked about and spun out of range.

Bullard glimpsed a damaged bomber banking to return to the German lines—an arc of gray smoke trailing it. A German fighter flashed in front of Bullard, blotting out his view of the bomber for an instant. In the distance, the bomber reappeared, erupted in a stupendous ball of flame and tumbled to earth in pieces.

Another Fokker flew by Bullard. Instinctively, he aimed his SPAD at the German plane and squeezed off some more rounds. In the distance, Bullard spied the other three bombers corkscrewing to earth, two of them on fire.

It was all over in just a couple of minutes. The German Fokkers disengaged and turned home. As the French planes headed back to their base, Bullard replayed the violent combat that he had just experienced. Everything had happened so fast. He noticed his hands were gripping the joystick tighter than usual. He ordered his hands to relax. His pounding heart settled down.

He felt Jimmy stirring in his flight jacket. "We made it, Jimmy." He stroked the monkey's head. "You're my good luck."

After safely landing, Bullard and the pilots quietly assembled in the camp's bar, awaiting the official reports. Two of their men had been shot down, it was announced. There was so much action going on, Bullard hadn't even noticed at the time.

The mechanics read their reports. Bullard's mechanic stated that Bullard's SPAD had fired 78 rounds and received seven bullet holes in its tail section. A sudden chill passed through Bullard. *Close!*

Commander Ménard approached Bullard. "Well done, Bullard," he said. "Now, you have been blooded with your first combat."

Most of the pilots headed for the mess hall, lost in thought about their fallen comrades. Bullard didn't feel much like talking as he followed the other pilots. On the mess hall bulletin board, he noticed his patrols the next day: 7–9 A.M. and 1–3 P.M. Bullard slowly picked at his tasteless meal.

BULLARD NEVER MISSED A flight patrol unless the weather grounded the planes. With each flight, his jitters lessened, and he grew more confident. He soon became an old-timer and part of a fierce fighting team. The other pilots felt safe flying with Bullard because they knew he was a good pilot. They knew he wouldn't run from a fight. And they knew he was itching to shoot down a German plane.

After six days of combat flying, Bullard was transferred on September 13 from Spa-93 to Spa-85, another crack squadron in the Lafayette Flying Corps. Spa-85 patrolled the Verdun sector in the region of Vadalaincourt and Bar-le-Duc.

One day, Bullard was patrolling his sector with his squadron near the German lines when a particularly aggressive formation of German Fokker triplanes appeared. Bullard didn't realize at the time the red-painted planes were part of the Richthofen Flying Circus—led by Baron von Richthofen—known as the most dangerous enemy pilot in the war. But Bullard could tell they were looking for a fight, and they were headed straight at him.

Bullard patted Jimmy inside his flying suit. "Here they come," he whispered. He armed his machine gun and gave his SPAD full throttle.

SHOT DOWN

The menacing red Fokkers flew straight at the French squadron, obviously looking for a fight. Bullard watched the lead plane for his signal. The captain motioned for combat maneuvers. The formation of French SPADs and Nieuports spun apart in wild gyrations, ready for battle.

The sky quickly swarmed with airplanes, each one trying to maneuver an enemy machine into its crosshairs. Bullard realized a triplane was headed directly at him, with staccato flashes of light and smoke erupting from its machine guns. Rivers of tracer bullets screamed past Bullard's SPAD.

Bullard mashed his right rudder pedal and heaved his stick to corkscrew down out of range. His agile plane instantly responded, pressing Bullard down in his seat. The taut reinforcing wires on his wings sang a higher pitch as he raced toward the earth.

Then, pulling up from below, Bullard fastened himself behind another Fokker. He fired short bursts from his Vickers machine gun. The Fokker wagged across the sky, trying to shake Bullard, but he stuck like a burr—firing bursts whenever the red plane swung across his crosshairs.

A short stream of bullets from Bullard's gun punched a line of holes across the Fokker's wings and fuselage. Pieces of wing fabric tore into strips and fluttered in the slipstream. The Fokker's engine belched smoke, then started sputtering and backfiring. The Fokker pilot made a slow, desperate turn away from the air battle. The plane began losing altitude. Bullard followed the crippled plane over the German lines to finish it off with another burst. He lined up the Fokker in his crosshairs. *My first kill. I can't miss—*

Bullard fired at the Fokker. Criss-crossing pencil lines of whitish smoke from tracer bullets streaked near Bullard's SPAD. German machine-gun crews on the ground were firing at Bullard in an effort to save their pilot. As soon as Bullard realized how low and vulnerable he was, he heard bullets thwap holes in the fabric of his plane. He heard the splang of bullets hitting metal parts. The SPAD shuddered and coughed. The controls felt mushy.

Bullard knew he was in serious trouble.

In the distance, Bullard noticed the smoking Fokker falling toward the ground in German territory. But he had no time to watch. He had to worry about himself now, or he would crash behind enemy lines.

After swinging his sputtering plane around toward the French lines, Bullard coaxed and willed the plane to stay aloft until he could find a safe landing spot. He finally made it over the enemy lines, but it still seemed like every German in the war was firing at him.

The SPAD's engine belched black smoke. Castor oil sprayed Bullard's windshield and face. He wiped his goggles with his sleeve and desperately tried to keep his engine running. A loud knock. The engine chugged one last time and died. Bullard had to land—now. The controls felt heavy. The SPAD hurtled toward the ground.

Bullard saw a muddy field in no-man's land appear ahead. The unnatural silence was broken only by the wind shrieking past the SPAD as it rapidly lost altitude. Bullard pushed away the cold fear that he wouldn't make the field. Shell-shattered trees passed ever closer beneath him. Bullard tore off his goggles; they might shatter on impact. He focused on the edge of the field. The ground came up fast. Then holding his breath, he carefully pulled back on his stick. *Keep enough airspeed. Don't stall. Don't stall. Keep the wings level. Don't hit a shellhole.*

The SPAD flared out a few feet above the ground and glided for a short distance. Its wheels thumped down. The plane bounced a few times. Its tail settled as it lost speed, and it finally came to rest. Bullard exhaled. *At least I didn't flip over.* He reached inside his jacket and stroked Jimmy's head. "You gave me good luck once more."

Bullets whizzed around the downed SPAD. Bullard quickly unfastened his seatbelt, clambered over the far side of his fuselage, and fell into a muddy shellhole. As long as the Germans were firing at him, he could only lie in the cold mud and listen to bullets puncturing his plane.

Hours dragged by. He shivered in his soaking wet clothes. Bullard felt Jimmy shivering, too. As darkness settled over no-man's land, the constant sniping at Bullard finally ended. Without warning, voices emerged from the remains of a forest behind him. Bullard whirled around. With a sigh of relief, he realized they were speaking French.

"Ah, Monsieur Bullard, I see you are still alive. And how is your son?" It was Bullard's aircraft mechanic. "We are here to transport you and your pathetic airplane back for repair."

A group of mechanics and soldiers with some horses appeared out of the shadows. The men tied Bullard's plane to a couple of horses and dragged it out of sight of the Germans. The mechanics quickly removed the SPAD's wings and set them aside. They lifted the fuselage onto a horse-drawn transport wagon, loaded the wings and tied everything down. Bullard and the mechanics hopped onto the back of a truck. They headed for the airfield a few miles away.

"I counted 96 holes in your machine, Bullard," Bullard's mechanic said. "None in you. You're a lucky man."

Bullard stroked Jimmy's head.

A CONFIRMED KILL

Bullard's life settled into a routine. If the weather was cooperative, he would fly a combat mission in the morning and another in the afternoon. But now it was a morning in November 1917—wintry cold and thick with clouds. Bullard thought he wouldn't be able to fly that day, so he rolled over in his warm cot and promptly fell back asleep.

All too soon, the duty sergeant shook him awake. "Get up, Bullard. You fly at 11."

Bullard wearily rose and stretched. Outside, the clouds were breaking up, allowing patches of blue sky to show through. He hurriedly dressed in his warmest flying gear and peeked into Jimmy's cage. Jimmy had been unusually quiet the last few days. He looked like he wasn't feeling well.

"I guess you can't go with me today, Jimmy," Bullard said. "But I'll be back soon. You get well."

In a few minutes, Bullard had fired up his SPAD, ready to do battle again with the Germans. At a signal the squadron roared down the airfield and launched themselves toward the Verdun battlefields.

At 12,000 feet, Bullard settled into the V-formation with his fellow pilots. As the planes droned toward the lines, they flew through puffy clouds dotting the sky. Bullard kept a sharp eye out for enemy planes. He was itching to do battle again. He was certain that he had shot down the red Fokker. But he didn't get a confirmed kill for it because the plane had crashed behind German lines, and no one else had seen him do it.

The air was rough. Bullard's plane bounced up and down as he threaded his way through clouds that constantly interrupted his view of the formation. He knew enemy planes could be hiding anywhere. He kept a constant lookout in all directions. Bullard patted his flight jacket. *It sure feels funny without Jimmy. I hope he doesn't have anything serious. He's been good luck so far.*

Bullard confronted a particularly large cloud and skirted around it. When he reached the other side, he suddenly realized he was alone in the sky. *Where are my wingmen?* He looked below and saw that he had crossed the Verdun battlefields. Bullard shivered. *It's really freezing today. Where is everyone?* The sound of the wind whooshing around his windshield and the constant roar of his engine made him feel even more alone. *Where are they?*

Finally, in the distance Bullard spotted a V-formation of seven planes. His heart leaped. *There they are! No . . . they're flying in the wrong direction. They're Germans!* The formation of Pfalz scout planes was flying 3,000 feet below him toward French-occupied territory. Thoughts of being alone instantly evaporated. Hope of a confirmed kill filled Bullard's mind.

The German formation kept flying straight and didn't make any unusual maneuvers. *Maybe they haven't seen me. Or maybe it's a trap.* Bullard scanned the sky in all directions. No other planes.

Bullard slipped into a large cloud to hide. White mist enveloped him, and rivulets of water streaked over his wings and fuselage. When he emerged, the Pfalzes had flown past him. As far as he could tell, they still hadn't seen him. Wary of a trap, Bullard took one more cautious look around before he pulled his throttle and shoved his stick forward.

Bullard's SPAD dove behind the last Pfalz in the German formation. Bullard triggered a burst of bullets from his Vickers—rat-tat-tat. The Pfalz pilot twisted around as a stream of tracers streaked past him. He looked startled to see Bullard's blue plane streaking toward him, with its machine gun blazing. The Pfalz swooped up in a loop to get behind Bullard.

Bullard threw his plane in a diving right bank and aimed for a nearby cloud to hide. The Pfalz completed its loop. The pilot must have expected to find a SPAD in front of him, but Bullard's plane was nowhere to be seen.

Emerging from his hiding place, Bullard saw the Pfalz above him. He shoved in his throttle and raced toward the enemy plane. As Bullard neared the Pfalz, he noted the black cross on the right side of its fuselage. The Pfalz centered in Bullard's gunsight. The German pilot saw the SPAD too late.

Bullard squeezed the trigger on his Vickers. He let off a

The Pfalz D.III, a German biplane fighter produced by Pfalz Flugzeugwerke, was an agile plane capable of high-speed diving attacks. The fuselage was a molded plywood monocoque design, which gave it great strength, light weight and a smooth, drag-reducing exterior. About 1,010 were built.

Crew: 1
Length: 22 ft 9 in
Wingspan: 30 ft 10 in
Height: 8 ft 9 in
Max takeoff weight: 2,061 lb
Engine: Mercedes D.IIIaü, 180 hp
Max speed: 115 mph
Service ceiling: 17,060 ft
Guns: 2 x 7.92 mm LMG 08/15 Spandau machine guns

long burst—rat-tat-tat-tat—and saw a line of holes march across the enemy plane toward the cockpit. The German pilot jerked as the bullets found his body. The Pfalz pitched up, did a slow roll to one side and fell toward the earth in a long spiral.

The deadly aerial duel took only a few moments. Before the other Pfalzes could engage Bullard in combat, he made a sharp bank and sped toward some large clouds. With his heart thumping, Bullard hid as long as he could. When he felt it was safe, he emerged and headed straight for home, still looking for his comrades.

There shouldn't be any doubt about this kill, he thought. The Pfalz had crashed on French territory.

Transferring to the American Flying Corps

For most of the war, the United States had remained neutral, but after a number of ships carrying Americans had been torpedoed by German submarines, diplomatic relations were broken off with Germany. Then, on April 6, 1917, the United States declared war on Germany. The first American troops arrived in France on June 26, 1917.

When Bullard heard that the Americans were coming to fight in France, he wondered if he would be able to transfer from the French Flying Service to the American Flying Service. Finally, in October, he heard that all American pilots flying for France would be accepted into the American Flying Service and promoted to the rank of lieutenant.

Bullard immediately went to Commandant Ménard's office, stood at attention, and snapped off a salute. "Permission to transfer to the American Flying Service, sir."

Ménard returned the salute. "At ease, Bullard." He shuffled

through some papers and grabbed one. "Ah, here we are." He cleared his throat. "Colonel Raynal Bolling, the commander-in-chief of the American Flying Service, has created a board to examine and approve the transfer of American pilots who fly for France." He looked at Bullard. "But it says you need to pass a physical." With a grin, he asked, "Do you think you think you can pass a physical?"

Bullard grinned back. "Yes, sir."

"Well, then, you have my permission—and my blessing. France will miss you." Ménard waved Bullard away. "I wish you well."

FLYING CONDITIONS WERE POOR in early October. Bullard used the opportunity to hop on a train to Paris to take his flying physical with other American pilots. Even though he had been poorly treated in his home country, he was still proud to be an American. He daydreamed about becoming a lieutenant—an officer—wearing an American aviator's uniform and fighting for his country as an American combat pilot.

After arriving in Paris, the pilots were examined by young American doctors in uniform. When it was Bullard's turn, he entered the examining room and saw four doctors busy reading his records on the table in front of them. He also noticed Dr. Gros, who didn't look particularly happy to see Bullard.

Bullard stood until one of the doctors looked up and asked, incredulously, "How did you ever learn to fly?"

What does he mean by that? Bullard wondered. He patiently explained how he had gone through pilot training with other Americans—the same training that all French military pilots had gone through to earn their wings. Bullard reminded the doctors that he received a flying certificate the previous May.

The doctors mumbled among themselves. One doctor rose and asked Bullard to sit on an exam stool. "Take off your boots," he ordered. He held Bullard's feet and closely examined them, flexing his ankles side-to-side. "Hmmm," he said. "You have flat feet."

"I served in the infantry and walked all over France," Bullard retorted. "No officer ever found my feet too flat to do that. Besides, I'm a pilot now, and I don't fly with my feet."

"I suppose you're right. Okay, open your mouth." The doctor pressed Bullard's tongue down with a tongue depressor and peered into his mouth. "Say 'ahhh.'"

"Ahhhh."

"Hmmm, it appears you have enlarged tonsils."

"Well, lucky for me, I'm not an opera singer," Bullard said. "You can see in my records I have never lost a day of duty because of a sore throat."

"Once again, I guess you're right," the doctor replied. "Next, we'll do a color-blindness test."

In the back of the room, Bullard heard Dr. Gros clear his throat and shuffle the papers in Bullard's file.

The young doctor interrupted Bullard's thoughts. "Here are some pictures of dots with colored numbers in them." He held a book in front of Bullard and flipped through the pages while Bullard correctly named all the numbers.

After a few more tests, the doctors announced that Bullard had passed the examination for becoming an American pilot. They would get in touch with Bullard when the necessary paperwork was processed.

Bullard was thrilled. As he headed back to the Spa-85

airfield with the other pilots, Bullard wondered how long it would be before he would be flying for his own country.

Bullard Receives His Orders

Unknown to Bullard, Colonel Bolling of the American Air Corps sent a message to the French Flying Service on October 21, 1917. The message ranked the 29 American pilots who had taken the physical examination and named those who had been approved for transfer whenever it was convenient for the French military.

Meanwhile, Bullard kept flying combat missions and saying goodbyes to his fellow pilots who, one-by-one, were called into Commandant Ménard's office over the next several days and given their American transfer papers.

At first, Bullard thought it would be only a matter of time before he was transferred, but it slowly began to dawn on him that all the transfers were given to white pilots. Still, his experience gave him an edge, he thought, and he did pass the physical exam.

Finally, in early November, Bullard was called to Ménard's office.

"At ease, Bullard," the commandant said. He held up a paper. "Bullard, here is a list of 29 pilots who have been graded by the Americans for transfer into their air corps. Only one pilot was rejected."

Bullard gasped.

"It wasn't you, Bullard. You did pass, but you ranked 28th out of 29—dead last for those who were accepted."

Bullard felt a sense of relief wash over him.

Ménard looked down at the paper. "Unfortunately, to fly for the Americans, you must be an officer." He frowned. "The others were promoted to lieutenant, but you were promoted only to sergeant." Ménard hesitated. "That means your transfer is denied. There is nothing I can do."

Bullard's knees felt weak as he left the office. Insulted and hurt by his own country rejecting him, Bullard tried to keep up his spirit by rationalizing that he was at least fighting on the same front as the American soldiers. In a way, he thought, he was doing his duty and serving the United States.

The weather turned bad again, so Bullard asked for a 24-hour leave with his mechanic to visit his friends, Kisling and White, in Paris. At the end of the Paris visit, the pair traveled to Bar-le-Duc and checked into the Café du Commerce. The small inn was near where they could catch the first morning train back to their airfield.

Bullard and one of his friends headed downstairs to the inn's restaurant for a cup of coffee and brandy. Being the only black person made Bullard stand out in the room crowded with soldiers. He elicited some curious looks, but he was used to that. One soldier, a captain, motioned for Bullard to come over and speak with him.

"Do you know that officer?" Bullard asked his companion.

"No. I've never seen him, but it sure looks like he wants to talk to you."

Bullard got up and walked over to the officer's table, stood at attention and saluted. The captain remained seated and didn't return the salute. Bullard knew the officer was violating military regulations, and he remained at attention.

The captain peppered Bullard with questions, but Bullard

remained silent. The officer yelled at Bullard, "Why don't you answer me?"

Bullard remained silent.

Livid with rage, the captain tried again, even louder. "Why don't you answer me?"

Bullard replied, "I can't answer you, sir, and I can't consider you an officer until you return my salute."

The captain jumped to his feet, insulting Bullard with a string of curses. He pointed at Bullard's medals. "You are unworthy of those decorations."

At last, a major at a nearby table who was watching the incident shouted at the captain to sit down and stop his disgusting behavior. The major took Bullard aside and explained that the captain had been commanding colonial troops in Africa and hadn't yet adjusted to the customs in France. "Please forget what happened. I will defend you if that officer tries to cause you any more trouble."

"It is forgotten, sir," Bullard said and saluted.

The major returned the salute. "Thank you. We are all French soldiers. *Vive la France.*" He clicked his heels and strode off.

Back at the airfield, Bullard tried to forget the unpleasant evening. But four days later, he received a letter from Dr. Gros. The correspondence stated that the doctor was disappointed that Bullard had quarreled with an officer and Bullard deserved whatever punishment might fall upon him. Bullard couldn't believe what he was reading. He lay back on his cot and wondered how in the world Dr. Gros—back in Paris—knew what had happened that night in Bar-le-Duc.

The next morning, the duty sergeant shook Bullard awake.

"Bullard, the flight doctor wants to see you."

Something was up. Bullard was sure of that.

The doctor told Bullard to sit down. "How is that leg of yours?"

"Fine," Bullard replied.

"Bullard, in the military we must sometimes take orders. I have been ordered to have you evacuated—released from combat duty."

Bullard was shocked. "Why?"

"I don't know, but I suspect the orders must be revenge for something you have done."

On November 11, 1917, Bullard was removed from the French Flying Service. He later transferred to his old unit—the 170th French Infantry. Because of his thigh wound, he was declared unfit for infantry combat duty and was sent to a military camp, Fontaine du Berger, 300 miles south of Paris. He performed menial tasks in a service battalion until the end of the war. To make matters worse, Bullard's Jimmy died during the great flu epidemic that swept the world in March 1918 and killed millions of people.

The Great War, as people called it, finally ended on November 11, 1918. More than 8 million soldiers and 6 million civilians had been killed. And 21 million soldiers had been wounded. Bullard was eventually demobilized from the military and headed for Paris.

He was about to start a new life.

6

Between the Wars

Paris

By the spring of 1919, Bullard was living in Paris and looking for a job. He began training as a boxer again, thinking that he might have a comeback in the ring—in spite of his head and thigh wounds from the war.

While training, Bullard kept his eyes open for other ways to make a living. He worked as a masseuse and an exercise trainer to an exclusive clientele that included many celebrities and prominent Parisians. Then he discovered that jazz bands springing up after the war were drawing large crowds at European nightclubs. When he noticed that black American jazz musicians were making good money in Paris, he decided to take lessons on playing the drums.

Bullard quickly mastered the basic techniques on drums. He was soon hired by a nightclub entrepreneur, an Italian named Joe Zelli, to play with a band in his club. By law, nightclubs had to close at midnight, but Zelli thought that if he could get an all-night license from the authorities, he could be very successful. If his club, Zelli's, was the only one open all night, it would surely draw tourists and Parisians who had plenty of money to spend.

At first, Zelli could not get a permit. But Bullard intervened on his behalf, using his influence and knowledge of French at the license bureau. In no time, Zelli had his permit. From then on, Zelli's opened at midnight after the other clubs had shut down for the evening and didn't close until after breakfast. Crowds packed the nightclub every night and spent small fortunes. The staff wore tuxedoes. So did the male customers. Women wore the latest Parisian fashions. Everyone wanted to go there.

Bullard played in one of the two bands at Zelli's. He enjoyed playing, but he still itched to fight. Zelli understood Bullard's desire to get back into the ring. And Zelli assured Bullard that he would always had a job at the club when he returned.

Taking Zelli at his word, Bullard signed a contract for two comeback fights in Egypt. He also signed a six-month contract to play with a jazz ensemble at the Hotel Claridge—a swank hotel in Alexandria, Egypt.

On December 21, 1921, he fought his first match in Egypt, which ended in a draw. His second bout, held on April 28, 1922, was a 15-round match against an Egyptian boxer who was at least 20 pounds heavier. During the fight, Bullard severely injured his right hand. The hand swelled up like a balloon, and Bullard had to mostly use his left jab. That match also ended in a draw. But Bullard was convinced he had won, in spite of the ruling from the referee—who just happened to be the boxer's brother-in-law.

Bullard's injured hand never healed correctly. He hung up his boxing gloves and never fought professionally again.

After Bullard returned to Paris, he became the band leader at Zelli's. Then he was promoted to manager and hired the entertainers who worked there. The club was a huge financial success by then. Regular customers included movie and stage stars, famous musicians, writers, politicians, and members of high-society.

One thing was lacking, though. Bullard wanted a family. During the war, his painter friends Kisling and White had introduced him to a young French girl—Marcelle Eugenie Henriette. Marcelle was from high society—the daughter of Louis Albert de Staumann and the Countess Helene Heloise Charlotte—so Bullard was surprised that he was still welcome to visit after the war.

Eventually, he asked Marcelle to go dancing. Love soon blossomed. After getting up the courage on the Fourth of July, 1922, Eugene approached Marcelle's parents. He told them of his love for their daughter. Albert and Helene Henriette laughed. "Our daughter has felt the same way about you for a long time."

A year later, on July 17, 1923, Eugene Bullard, age 28, married Marcelle Henriette, who was 22, at the city hall in Paris. Marcelle's parents threw an elaborate wedding party that attracted people from all walks of life. The wedding caused a sensation—not because of the difference in the couple's color—but because of their difference in social standing.

The Bullards honeymooned for two weeks on the southern coast of France at the fashionable resort of Biarritz, not far from Spain. The couple returned to Paris and settled in a luxurious apartment with a view of the Eiffel Tower. Eleven months later, on June 6, 1924, their first daughter—Jacqueline Jeanette Marcelle Bullard—was born. In October 1926, their only son—Eugene, Jr.—was born, but six months later he died of pneumonia. The following year, in December 1927, their second daughter—Lolita Josephine Bullard—was born.

Bullard took his family responsibility seriously and pondered how he could be a better provider.

He decided to aim for something even bigger than managing a club.

SNUBS AND SUCCESSES

In 1928, Bullard bought the small, triangular-shaped Le Grand Duc nightclub from its current owner, Ada Louise Smith. Known to everyone as "Bricktop," she was a red-headed, light-skinned black singer and dancer from the south side of Chicago. Bricktop was a favorite of American songwriter Cole Porter, who helped make her one of the stars of Paris. Eventually she became world-famous.

Bullard was determined to make a success of his club. At first, many of Bullard's musician friends played at his club for no money, just to return the favors he had given them over the years. As business picked up, Bullard hired a number of famous entertainers, making his nightclub a favorite attraction for the rich and famous. On a typical night, his patrons might include movie stars like Charlie Chaplin and Edward G. Robinson, artists like Pablo Picasso, or writers like F. Scott Fitzgerald and Ernest Hemingway. (The black drummer in Hemingway's *The Sun Also Rises* was likely based on Bullard.) Even Edward, the Prince of Wales, was a regular when he was in Paris. Le Grand Duc was *the* place to be seen.

Each year, Bullard arranged for an African American band to play a free concert during the nurses' graduation dance at the American Hospital in Paris. He wanted to express his thanks for how well the hospital treated the local musicians and artists.

The free concerts were a big hit with the staff doctors and nurses. They all thanked Bullard profusely for his services—except for one hospital administrator. Dr. Gros—the American doctor who had engineered Bullard's transfer and demotion from the French Flying Service—mostly ignored Bullard by pretending not to know him.

In June 1928, Bullard learned from Lt. Ted Parsons, an old flying friend, that a monument honoring the Escadrille Lafayette and the Lafayette Flying Corps had been erected in a Paris suburb not far from Versailles. The dedication ceremony was scheduled for July Fourth. Every American aviator of the corps had been invited, except Bullard.

Bullard was determined to see the ceremony, so he went anyway—invitation or not. The impressive white, stone memorial he saw was composed of a central arch upon which the names of dead American pilots were inscribed. Under the monument was a sanctuary crypt holding 68 sarcophagi, which held the remains of dead pilots.

From his vantage point, Bullard saw Dr. Gros waiting in the reviewing stand with other French officials. Dr. Gros, the president of the Board of the Memorial Association, came forward when the ceremony began and formally presented the monument to France.

The American ambassador, Myron T. Herrick, then spoke, referring to criticism about the late entrance of the United States in the war:

"During three terrible years, when the sting of criticism cut into every American soul, these pilots were showing the world how their countrymen could fight if they were only allowed the opportunity. To many of us they seemed to be the saviors of our national honor, giving the lie to current sneers upon the courage of the nation."

After the ceremony, Bullard lined up with the other Corps members to shake hands with the officials. Dr. Gros was forced to shake Bullard's hand, but he didn't look happy.

Sometime later, Bullard discovered the French government had also given scrolls of gratitude to Dr. Gros for distribution to every American pilot who had flown for France during the war. Bullard was the only pilot who didn't receive one.

It became obvious to Bullard that—in the end—Dr. Gros had once again gotten his way. Bullard made a silent vow that he would keep trying to get the scroll that rightfully belonged to him.

For now, though, he had to turn his attention to his business and his family.

Nightclubs and Spies

By the early 1930s, Bullard sold Le Grand Duc. He was successful enough, though, to purchase another nightclub named L'Escadrille and a gymnasium he named Bullard's Athletic Club.

Bullard posed for muscleman-type photos that were included in advertisements for his athletic club, which listed boxing lessons, massage, whirlpool baths and even ping-pong. Catering to men, women and children, Bullard's club attracted both Parisians and foreigners. They appreciated his style and his fluency in French. And that included Jeff Dickson, who had bet Bullard he couldn't become a pilot. Dickson had become

BULLARD'S ATHLETIC CLUB

(Ex-Entraîneur de DIXIE-KID, ex-Champion du Monde, poids Welter
et de AL. BROWN, Champion du Monde, Entraîneur de YOUNG PEREZ)

15, Rue MANSART, PARIS-9ᵉ

Tél. : PIGALLE 70-05

SON GYMNASE UNIQUE à PARIS

· de 8 m. de hauteur, entièrement vitré
AIR, LUMIÈRE, TOUT CONFORT
(Cabines d'habillage et Placards individuels)

CULTURE PHYSIQUE

HOMMES · FEMMES · ENFANTS

BOXE - MASSAGE

PING-PONG -- HYDROTHÉRAPIE

OUVERT TOUS LES JOURS DE 8 H. A 20 H. 30
Location de la Salle et Cours d'ensemble à Sociétés

Bullard eventually opened an athletic club in Paris, where he sponsored wrestling matches and other sports.

a boxing promoter, and he trained his boxers at Bullard's.

After eight years, Bullard separated from his wife. They divorced in December 1935, their differences in social status and likes and dislikes finally becoming too much for the marriage. In 1936, Bullard received custody of 12-year-old Jacqueline and 9-year-old Lolita. His daughters received the finest education and attended a private school south of Paris. All of this cost Bullard a lot of money.

Luckily, Bullard's nightclubs hadn't been affected very much by the Great Depression. His new L'Escadrille club was always packed with customers, making him financially secure. And his athletic club attracted many famous people, including trumpeter Louis Armstrong and pianist Fats Waller, who liked to exercise after patronizing Bullard's nightclub.

Life seemed good for Bullard, but for a number of years the French military intelligence had been closely monitoring events in nearby Germany. Adolf Hitler had strengthened the German military and taken over Austria and Czechoslovakia by force. The French government believed that Germany once more wanted war with France.

Early in 1939, Bullard was approached by Inspector George Leplanquais. He spoke with Bullard in the nightclub office.

"Eugene," the inspector said, shutting the office door, "you know how to speak German. Would you agree to listen in on conversations from your German customers and tell me about any suspicious activities?" Before Bullard could answer, the inspector interrupted. "Think before you answer because if you agree, you can never change your mind."

"Before I answer you," Bullard said, "will my daughters be safe?"

Without hesitation, Inspector Leplanquais replied, "You have my word, Bullard."

"In that case, my answer—of course—is yes."

"*Trés bien,* Bullard. You have our gratitude."

"One thing, inspector," Bullard said. "I've seen a young blonde hanging around German customers in my club. I'm beginning to think she's a German sympathizer or maybe even a spy."

Inspector Leplanquais chuckled. "You're half right, Eugene. She's a spy by the name of Cleopatre Terrier. She works for us, and you'll be working with her."

In a few days, Bullard was introduced to Terrier, an attractive 27-year-old Alsatian woman who was fiercely anti-

German. "Call me Kitty," she said. Fluent in German, French, and English, Terrier was working with the French to avenge her father who had been killed by the Germans in the Great War.

From then on, whenever Bullard was near a table with Germans he would listen intently but unobtrusively. At the time, German patrons believed they were members of a master race, and they never suspected a black man could understand their language. If Bullard heard any useful information, he mentioned it to Terrier, who could slip away without notice and report to the authorities.

Meanwhile, underneath all this intrigue, criminal groups similar to the Mafia were actively extorting protection money from Parisian nightclubs. On July 2, 1939, Bullard entered L'Escadrille in the early morning hours, expecting to see his club packed as usual and jumping with activity. But only two patrons were hanging out at the bar.

Bullard looked stunned. "What's going on—"

The bartender held his finger up to his lips and pointed toward the men's room.

Bullard entered the restroom and saw a Corsican gang member named Justin Perretti reflected in the mirrors. He was swaying and cursing like a madman.

"What's wrong, Justin?" Bullard asked.

"You know what's wrong," Perretti replied. "And I'm going to take care of it—and you!"

Bullard thought Perretti was just drunk. Bullard grabbed his arms, held them behind him and marched him out the front door, knocking over a vase of flowers on the piano in the process. Bullard certainly didn't need a drunk driving off his business. But a little while later, Perretti showed up again and immediately went into the restroom again.

Bullard confronted Perretti again. "Why'd you come back?"

Perretti answered by whipping out a large knife and lunging at Bullard. He sidestepped, knocked the knife out of Perretti's hand and again marched him outside onto the sidewalk.

"This is your last night on earth, Bullard," Perretti said. He brushed off his sleeves. "How about calling me a taxi?"

The doorman called a taxi, and Perretti drove off. Bullard hoped it was the last he'd see of him, at least until he was sober. Bullard turned his attention to mopping up the water that had spilled inside his piano. Half an hour later, Bullard looked up and saw a crazed-looking Perretti pointing a Luger pistol at him.

"I'm going to kill you, Bullard."

Bullard slowly walked toward Perretti, trying to calm him down. As soon as Bullard got close enough, he slapped Perretti's gun arm down just as the gun fired. Pain stabbed Bullard in his stomach.

Bullard grabbed Perretti, holding his gun arm behind his back and wrestling him to the floor. Perretti kept firing and shot himself in the back. A customer threw a bottle to Bullard. He caught it and pounded Perretti on the head with the bottle, fracturing his skull.

Customers screamed for Bullard to stop, "You're killing him!"

Bullard finally realized what he was doing and tossed the bottle aside. He stood up. His stomach was really burning. Blood ran down his right leg, soaking his pants. Customers hailed a taxi, and Bullard sped off to the nearest hospital.

"Bullard," the doctor said, "I think your intestines and

internal organs have been punctured. The bullet entered your stomach and came out your right hip. We cannot repair the damage. There is nothing we can do." The doctor handed a note to a nurse. "We will observe you for 24 hours, but you cannot eat or drink anything."

Late the next day, the doctor looked in on Bullard. He sounded amazed that Bullard was still alive. "How do you feel?"

"Hungry."

The doctor laughed. "You won't die, will you?" He ordered a small portion of baby food and mashed potatoes. "Let's see how you do."

By the next day, Bullard was complaining that he wanted some real food, so each day he was given a bit more to eat. On the fifth day in the hospital, Bullard successfully insisted on his discharge. He wanted to return home to recover there.

While Bullard was in the hospital, Terrier had returned to Paris after an assignment. She was investigating the shooting and had discovered some interesting information about Perretti, but she couldn't visit Bullard in the hospital for fear of arousing suspicion. After he was released, though, Terrier informed Bullard that Perretti—although a gangster—was fiercely pro-French and anti-German.

Perretti had thought Bullard was a German sympathizer because he understood German too well and was spending too much time around his German customers. In his drunken condition, Perretti thought Bullard was an enemy agent, and it was his patriotic duty to kill him.

Bullard suddenly felt terrible. He wondered if both Perretti and he were working for the French Underground. He hoped Perretti would live.

A week later, Leplanquais and a group of policemen showed up at Bullard's apartment. "You've done very well," Leplanquais said. "You are now a full member of the Underground."

Bullard hesitated. "What about my daughters if the Germans occupy Paris? They could kill Jacqueline and Lolita because of my Underground membership."

"Tut, tut. Remember, we promised to take care of them if anything happens to you. It's a promise we will keep."

"In that case, I will do my best," Bullard replied. "I look forward to continue working with you."

WAR BREAKS OUT AGAIN

On September 1, 1939, German forces attacked Poland. Two days later, France and Great Britain declared war on Germany because they had alliances with Poland.

By October, Germany completely occupied Poland. As a precaution against German air attacks, French authorities imposed nightly blackouts in Paris at sundown. American officials ordered American citizens without urgent business in Paris to return to the United States. Bullard wasn't about to leave, however. He was committed to his Underground espionage work even though he knew the Germans would kill him if they discovered he was a spy.

Bullard was now even more concerned about his daughters, who attended school south of Paris. He wanted their company, so he removed them from school and brought them home. By the time Jacqueline and Lolita arrived home in early 1940, Bullard's business had fallen off drastically because of the nightly blackouts. Most foreigners and their money had left Paris. Bullard was forced to close both his nightclub and gymnasium.

Bullard's money was dwindling fast and expenses were piling up. He was pleased when the wealthy widow, Mrs. June Jewitt James, invited him to work for her. Mrs. James also invited Bullard and his daughters to live at her large château in Neuilly—an offer he gratefully accepted.

Bullard worked for her as a chauffeur and masseur. He answered the phones and made sure all the rooms were clean. At the many formal dinners Mrs. James gave for French and American dignitaries, he also worked as a waiter. On those occasions, he would wear his dress uniform displaying all his medals.

One day, a champagne luncheon was scheduled to honor Mrs. James's official donation of many ambulances she had purchased for France. American and French flags flew high on poles above her mansion. Among the many guests was Dr. Gros, who was still the administrator at the local hospital.

Dr. Gros motioned to Bullard, who was dressed in his uniform and carrying a tray of drinks. The doctor selected a glass of champagne and examined Bullard. Normally, Dr. Gros would have pretended not to know him, but this time he spoke. "Bullard," he said, pointing to a medal, "I didn't know you had the Medaille Militaire."

Bullard stiffened and sarcastically answered, "Oh, I thought you kept all my records—just as you kept the scroll that was issued to me and every other member of the Flying Corps by the French government."

Dr. Gros's jaw tightened. He looked like he was going to say something. His face flushed red. He turned and walked away.

That felt good, Bullard thought. *I hope I never see that man again.* He tried to put Dr. Gros out of his mind as he continued serving drinks.

RESISTANCE

A few weeks after the champagne luncheon and Bullard's encounter with Dr. Gros, Inspector Leplanquais ordered him back to Paris. "Bullard, you are now in the Resistance effort fighting against Germans instead of merely gathering information."

Bullard nodded and listened intently.

"The Germans have invaded northeastern France. Millions of refugees are moving south toward Paris."

Grim-faced, Bullard wasn't totally convinced that the Germans could actually take Paris. But he would make sure Terrier, his Underground partner, took care of his teenage daughters while he did his part in the fight against the Germans.

"I'm not one to run away from a fight, Inspector. I'm going to rejoin my old outfit—the 170th Infantry. I heard they're about a hundred miles east of Paris."

"Ah, Bullard. It will be their gain, our loss. Good luck."

At his apartment, Bullard loaded a knapsack with canned food, sausages and bread. His daughters also included the two-volume history of the Lafayette Flying Corps, which mentioned him. He contacted Terrier and made sure his daughters had enough food and supplies before he left. Then, after stuffing some money in his pocket, Bullard set out to find his old infantry regiment. He took the subway as far as Porte D'Italie on the edge of Paris and then set out on foot. Joining other soldiers headed toward the lines, he walked all day and night, fighting against the tide of terrified civilians fleeing in the opposite direction.

Some of the refugees told Bullard that the Germans had already captured the area that he was headed for. There was no sense in continuing toward the lines. After a day and a half of walking, a weary Bullard turned around and headed back to Paris. It took another three days and nights before he reached Porte D'Italie where he had originally departed Paris for the front lines.

French police were waiting. "You cannot enter," they informed Bullard and the other refugees trying to enter Paris. "We are under orders to stop everyone."

How would he tell his daughters that he was okay? He tried to sneak into the city at several different points, but was always turned away. Rumors spread that the French 51st Infantry was fighting south of Paris. Bullard finally decided to head there and join in the battle.

Hordes of people fleeing southward filled the roads. Bullard joined them, diving for cover whenever a German Stuka flew over and dropped bombs on the refugees. After more than a day and 50 miles, the town of Chartres came into sight.

By chance, Bullard spied a familiar black face among the refugees. It was a friend named Bob Scanlon, a boxer and fellow legionnaire in the last war. Bullard didn't feel so alone anymore. The two arrived in Chartres near the busy railroad station, which had Red Cross railcars filled with wounded French soldiers headed for hospitals across France.

Without warning, the sky filled with the high-pitched shrieks of diving Stukas and the whistling of bombs. Explosions erupted around the station, tossing debris into the air and twisting rails like pretzels.

Bullard threw himself on the ground. Scanlon dove into a crater about 20 feet away. A terrible flash of heat and a tremendous boom washed over Bullard. As the Stukas flew off, Bullard lifted his head and looked for his friend. Nothing but smoke rose from the hole where Scanlon had sought safety. Bullard ran over to the crater, dumbstruck. Nothing was there. Absolutely nothing.

Horrors surrounded Bullard. Body parts lay scattered everywhere. A woman's body lay nearby—sliced in half. Her child shrieked, "Mama! Mama!"

Bullard left for Orleans, experiencing even more horrors along the road. People fought each other for any scrap of food or drop of water. Women gave birth alongside the road. When people had to answer nature's call, they did openly without any privacy—there simply was none. No one noticed, anyway. Everyone was just trying to stay alive.

On June 15, Bullard reached Orleans and offered his services at the temporary barracks of the 51st Infantry.

The commanding officer appeared. He stared at Bullard. "Bullard! Is that you?"

Bullard stared back at the officer. "Major Bader!"

They embraced.

Bullard stepped back. "I haven't seen you since Verdun, Major Bader. You were a lieutenant then."

"And you were a corporal manning a machine gun." Major Bader rubbed his chin for a second. "And you will man one again. I'm assigning you to a machine gun company on the south side of the Loire River. You must hold back the Germans on the north side."

That night, Bullard and his machine gun company fought valiantly, holding back the Germans until midnight. Heavy German artillery then bombarded Orleans, set it on fire and forced the French soldiers to retreat. For the next three days, the French kept falling back and defending more towns, only to be driven off by the more mobile German infantry.

On June 18, Bullard and the 51st Infantry reached the old French town of Le Blanc, under heavy artillery fire from huge German 88mm cannons. Bullard saw a scene of utter devastation and ruin. The continuous bombardment shook the ground and flung debris and dirt high into the sky.

Bullard carried a light machine gun and cautiously entered a street with some other soldiers. He heard a familiar whistling sound. Then nothing. A blinding flash of light. A deafening explosion. The powerful blast lifted Bullard into the air and flung him across the street.

He didn't feel the shrapnel shard when it gouged the skin over his right eye. He didn't feel his spine fracture. But he felt a terrible blow when he landed and his head smashed into a wall.

When he came to, he discovered that 11 of his comrades had been killed and 16 wounded from the shell that had exploded. If his head hadn't glanced off the wall at an angle that had softened the blow, he knew he would have been one of the dead, too.

The next day, Bullard found he couldn't fight any longer. He was in intense pain. His neck and back hurt, and he had a gash in his forehead.

Major Bader feared Bullard would be executed by the Nazis because he was black, a member of the French Resistance, and a hero of the Great War. Bullard was ordered to leave France for Spain through Biarritz. There he would be safe—for the time being.

"Here's a safe-conduct pass, Bullard." The major handed him some paperwork. "Good luck. But you must leave immediately."

Bullard grabbed a rifle for a crutch and hobbled toward Spain.

BULLARD HEADED FOR THE town of Angoulême about a day's journey on his way toward Biarritz, where he hoped he could find safe passage into neutral Spain. He walked the best he could, leaning on his rifle. He fought shooting pain as he slowly took each step. Eventually, it dawned on him that if he were captured with a gun, he would be instantly shot. He found a large stick to use as a cane and tossed his rifle into some bushes.

Because Bullard was wearing his uniform and medals, the occasional truck heading in his direction would offer him a lift. Twenty-four hours later, Bullard saw the French town of Angoulême and its military hospital appear in the distance. And none too soon, Bullard thought. His pain was so intense, he couldn't walk much farther.

Bullard finally made it into the hospital, which was filled with wounded men. By an astounding coincidence, Bullard knew the doctor on duty: Dr. H. C. de Vaux, who had been a medic at Verdun. Dr. Vaux was also one of the grateful doctors at the American Hospital in Paris where Bullard and other musicians had played at no cost.

"Bullard," Dr. Vaux said, "I can't believe it's you."

Bullard couldn't believe it, either. He sat down while Dr. de Vaux examined him.

"Your spine is misaligned and you have a split vertebra." The doctor picked up a syringe and injected Bullard with a painkiller. He wrapped Bullard's back tightly with bandages. "This will help support your spine." Finally, he placed a bandage over Bullard's right eye.

The doctor sat down and looked earnestly at him. "It's too dangerous for you here. And you can't go back to Paris. You must get out of France as soon as possible." He gave Bullard some fresh water and six cans of sardines. "Good luck. I'm sorry, but I must look after the other wounded now." The doctor shook Bullard's hand and walked away.

On the road, Bullard traded three cans of his sardines for a soldier's bicycle and pedaled toward Biarritz. In the early hours of June 22, he found the American consulate office and took a place in line with other waiting Americans. He stretched out on the ground to sleep until the consulate opened.

McWilliams, the American consul, arrived and opened the office early. When Bullard's turn came, McWilliams questioned him and discovered who he actually was. "You'd better get out of that uniform," McWilliams said. "There are German military officers in the area staying at my hotel and, if they see you . . ."

Hearing about Bullard's dilemma, other Americans in line offered him a shirt and trousers. Bullard quickly changed into civilian clothes.

"Okay, now give me your passport," McWilliams ordered.

"Passport?" Bullard looked stricken. "I don't have a passport. Americans didn't need passports when I came to France."

"Then how can we prove you're an American?" The consul tapped his head. "Where were you born?"

"Columbus, Georgia."

"I've visited there. What river flows through Columbus?"

"The Chattahoochee."

"What's the name of the town across the river?"

"Phenix City if you turn right, Girard if you turn left."

"Hmm. Wait over there." The consul pointed to a chair.

While Bullard sat awaiting his fate, two Americans he knew appeared in line—Colonel Sparks of the American Legion in Paris and R. Craine Gartz, one of his massage clients. The two Americans spoke with McWilliams and confirmed Bullard's American citizenship.

"Okay," the consul said, "that's good enough for me, but you'll have to get your passport at the Office of the Consul General in Bordeaux. And you'll have to leave your identification papers here in case the Germans grab you." He handed Bullard a passport application.

Bullard knew that Bordeaux was about 100 miles away, but what else could he do? He hopped on his bicycle and pedaled for two days and nights until he reached the consulate, in great pain and totally exhausted. He slept for a few hours and finally met with the American consul. After the consul took Bullard's photograph, he was issued a passport and given $20 from the American government.

When Bullard left the consulate, it was late in the afternoon. His bicycle was missing. He took another bicycle and headed back to Biarritz, arriving there the night of June 29. He thought it ironic that it wouldn't be long before the Germans would be enjoying the beaches in Biarritz where he had once honeymooned.

The next day, Bullard had a stroke of luck. He caught a ride with an old friend, who was driving an ambulance filled with Americans trying to leave France. Unfortunately, the roads were so filled with traffic they could get only as far as the small French seaport town of St. Jean de Luz. By the afternoon of the next day, they made their way at last to the French town of Hendaye and the International Bridge into Spain where safety and escape lay.

Then Bullard ran into yet another old friend and ex-legionnaire who was working for the Spanish customs office. Bullard's old comrade expedited his entry into Spain, but it wasn't until the wee hours of the next morning, July 2, when Bullard actually set foot on Spanish soil.

After resting for several days in a hotel reserved by the Red Cross, Bullard boarded a train for Lisbon, Portugal. The American steamship, *Manhattan*, was waiting there to transport hundreds of Americans back home.

On July 12, 1940, Bullard embarked for the United States—a land he hadn't seen in 30 years.

As Bullard watched Europe recede into the distance, he wondered if he would ever see his daughters again.

7

New York

America

Six days later, the *Manhattan* arrived in New York. Bullard was thrilled to see the Statue of Liberty pass by as his ship headed for the docks. He hoped the attitudes in America had changed in the years he had lived overseas.

Jack Spector, the former commander of the Paris American Legion Post, was waiting at the dock to greet the arriving American veterans of the Great War. Bullard belonged to that post, so he listened with great interest as Spector talked to the veterans who had gathered around him.

"I have arranged hotel reservations for all of you," Spector announced. Turning to Bullard, he tried to hide a smirk. "That is, except for you, Bullard. I didn't know you were with the group."

Bullard was crestfallen. *I guess things haven't changed that much.* Fortunately, a fellow soldier on the ship gave him a few dollars to rent a room. That night Bullard stayed in a room on Seventh Avenue, but eventually he found an apartment at 80 East 116th Street in Harlem, where he took up permanent residence.

One of Bullard's first jobs was working as a security guard

in Brooklyn at a U.S. Army base. He traveled to work every day on a ferry that carried a number of government workers. As the ferry was docking one day, the passengers crowded forward to exit the boat. A white worker thought Bullard was taking too long. He pushed Bullard forward and yelled, "You black bastard!"

Bullard swung and knocked the worker down. As the swearing worker got to his feet, the angry crowd closed in on Bullard. He thought he might actually get killed.

Suddenly, a man stepped in front of Bullard and yelled "Stop!" He flashed an F.B.I. badge. "I saw everything. This white man insulted the black man. Go ashore and go to work."

The agent turned his attention to the white man. "And you—you apologize to this man. He's fought Germans for you and has won more medals than you or your family will get in a lifetime."

Bullard realized then that it was probably the F.B.I.'s business to know everything about every government worker. The other worker meekly apologized to Bullard.

The agent let the man go on his way and turned to Bullard. "Those kind of people make me sick. Is there anything else I can do for you?"

"How about a job as a longshoreman at the navy base on Staten Island? They get paid a lot more than I do."

The next day, Bullard had a job as a longshoreman. The job required heavy lifting, which was very painful for Bullard, but he would need the extra money to support his daughters if he could somehow bring them to New York. He hadn't heard anything from Jacqueline or Lolita, though, and he worried about them every day.

By the fall of 1940, Bullard felt it was time for action to get his daughters. He traveled by train to Washington, D.C. and presented his case to officials. They promised to take up his cause. Bullard traveled back to New York and waited impatiently for news.

In January 1941, Bullard received two telegrams stating that arrangements were being made to transport his daughters to the United States. He was ecstatic. He read and re-read the telegrams.

Finally, on a cold, snowy February 3, the *Exeter* arrived at a Jersey City dock with Lolita and Jacqueline—now 14 and 16 years old. With tears in his eyes, Bullard hugged and kissed his daughters. He hadn't seen them for almost a year. He took them home to New York to learn English and continue their schooling.

Bullard had been worried for a long time about his daughters trapped in France. He had been through terrible ordeals while fighting in France and trying to escape. And his spinal injury gave him great pain. He needed a well-earned rest, so in March of 1941 he checked into a French hospital in New York that treated veterans of the Great War.

While lying in bed in the hospital, Bullard was startled one day by a knock on his door. "Come in."

Bob Scanlon stood in the doorway.

The last time Bullard saw Scanlon, he thought Scanlon was killed by a bomb in Chartres. "It can't be," he exclaimed. "You're supposed to be dead. Are you a ghost?"

"No." Scanlon grinned. "Somehow I survived that blast with only minor injuries. I was thrown clear, and when I came to, you were gone."

"I can't believe it. Sit down and let's talk."

In the early summer, Bullard was released from the hospital and he returned to work.

In the fall of 1942, an invitation arrived at Bullard's apartment for a dinner at the New York Paris Hotel. The special event was for Paris American Legion members. Bullard was still a member, and he looked forward to attending the dinner. Shortly before the event, however, he received an anonymous letter mailed from New York and postmarked November 22:

> Dear Comrade,
>
> Your extended sojourn abroad has perhaps made you forget that in the States white and colored people do not mix at social functions.
>
> It would be to your advantage not to attend the dinner on Monday night or to join in any social activities of Paris Post No. 1 in the future.

Infuriated, Bullard sent a copy of the letter to Jack Spector—the former Paris American Legion Post commander—who had slighted Bullard on the dock when he arrived from France. Bullard expressed his dismay at the insult, but he never received any acknowledgment. Not one to back down, though, Bullard left his daughters at home and attended the dinner—which thankfully ended without any incidents.

AFTER WWII ENDED IN 1945, Bullard decided to visit his hometown of Columbus, Georgia. While in France, he had heard his brother had been lynched over a land dispute, but he thought he might find some other family members still living there.

Bullard discovered that his house and others had been torn down to make way for apartment buildings. He couldn't find any of his brothers or sisters. And while he was visiting Columbus, he was treated poorly. Disappointed at how things hadn't changed, Bullard left Georgia for New York and never returned.

THROUGH THE YEARS, BULLARD found himself involved in other racial confrontations. In the late summer of 1949, he was beaten by police who were guarding a concert in a park outside New York.

And when Bullard boarded a bus in the Peekskill Mountains, the driver told him to "sit in the rear." Bullard refused. The driver insulted him and then he threw a punch at the driver, and a fistfight erupted. The driver punched Bullard in the face several times, injuring his left eye. He lost most of the sight in that eye and had to wear glasses from then on.

Bullard toured Europe for a while as an interpreter for Louis Armstrong. In 1954, he was invited by the French government—all expenses paid—to the Bastille Day ceremonies in Paris. Bullard and other French war veterans relit the eternal flame at the Tomb of the Unknown Soldier. He also placed a wreath of flowers beside the tomb under the Arc de Triomphe.

Five years later, on Bullard's 64th birthday—October 9, 1959—he was in the New York French Consulate on Fifth Avenue. The occasion was a formal ceremony to honor Bullard's distinguished military and civilian service to France. The French consul pinned a Legion of Honor medal on Bullard's lapel—his fifteenth medal—which made him a Knight of the Legion of Honor.

Bullard places a wreath at France's Tomb of the Unknown Soldier under the Arc de Triomphe in Paris, 1954.

His daughters and other dignitaries heard Bullard proudly say in French: "I have served France the best I could. France taught me the true meaning of liberty, equality and fraternity. My services to France can never repay all I owe her."

By that time of his life, Bullard was working as an elevator operator in Rockefeller Center. He always wore his medals on his elevator uniform. Producers of NBC's *Today Show*, headquartered in the building, took notice. They arranged for Bullard to be interviewed on television by host Dave Garroway. Bullard described his war years to the viewers and told the viewers how he earned the 15 medals that he held up in a case for the camera.

Host Dave Garroway interviewed Bullard, appearing in his Rockefeller Center elevator operator's uniform, on NBC's Today Show *in New York City. Garroway showed off Bullard's medals to the studio audience.*

In the spring of 1960, Bullard received an invitation:

> General de Gaulle, President of the French Republic, and Madame de Gaulle, request Mr. Eugene Jacques Bullard to do them the honor of being present at the reception which they are giving at the Armory of the Seventh Infantry Regiment, 643 Park Avenue, at 4:45 P.M., Tuesday, April 26th.

Bullard was thrilled. He dressed in his Legion uniform,

wearing all 15 of his medals. When he showed up at the Armory, he was ushered to a table reserved for VIPs.

At 6 P.M., President Charles de Gaulle appeared and gave a brief speech to the large crowd of French notables and Americans who had served France. After his speech, de Gaulle embraced a number of people. Noticing Bullard, he offered his hand, drew him close, and embraced him.

This is the proudest moment of my life, Bullard thought.

Bullard's medals (left to right): French Aviator Badge, Légion d'Honneur Chevaliers, Médaille Militaire, Croix de Guerre with Bronze Star, Croix du Combattant Volontaire, Croix du Combattant, Médaille des Engages Volontaires WWII, Médaille de la Victoire 1914–1918, Médaille Commemorative Française 1914–1918, Médaille des Forces Française Libres, Insigne des Blessés Militaire, Médaille des Verdun, Médaille des Somme, Médaille des Engagés Volontaires WWI, American Volunteer.

Epilogue

The Final Battle

In early 1961, Bullard started feeling sharp pains in his stomach. Thinking the pains were from ulcers, he tried to ignore them. The pain finally became so intense, his family persuaded him to have medical tests at New York's Metropolitan Hospital. Exploratory surgery revealed that he had advanced intestinal cancer.

Bullard entered Metropolitan Hospital on August 18 for treatment. He received visitors while wearing his yellow silk pajamas. Propped up on two pillow with needles stuck in his body, he told one friend, "The sooner I die, the sooner the suffering will be over."

He allowed physicians to treat him with experimental drugs, but it was to no avail. "I'm not afraid of dying," Bullard said. "God is my friend. He has always been my friend."

By October 12, Bullard's condition required an oxygen tube down his throat. He slipped in and out of consciousness. Mrs. Connell, a friend who was typing his memoirs, arrived to tell him she had finished the last page.

Bullard struggled to breathe. He opened his eyes and noticed how distressed his friend appeared. Bullard withdrew the tube from his throat and smiled. "Don't fret, honey. It's easy."

Mrs. Connell ran for a nurse to replace his oxygen tube. Bullard received last rites from a priest. He died four hours later at 10:10 P.M.

EUGENE JACQUES BULLARD, HERO of the French Foreign Legion and the Lafayette Flying Corps, was buried in a military service, wearing a freshly pressed French Foreign Legion uniform. The flag of France was draped over his coffin.

Bullard's final resting place is Grave No. 7, Plot 53 of the Federation of French War Veterans Cemetery in Flushing, New York. His grave is marked by a simple square inscribed with his name, birth date, and the date of his death.

On September 14, 1994, the United States Air Force posthumously commissioned Eugene Jacques Bullard as a second lieutenant. On October 9, 1994, Governor Zell Miller declared a "Eugene Bullard Day" in Georgia.

To all who shall see these presents, greeting:

Know ye, that reposing special trust and confidence in the patriotism, valor, fidelity and abilities of **Eugene J. Bullard**, I do appoint HIM, SECOND LIEUTENANT (POSTHUMOUSLY) in the

United States Air Force
(FORMALLY AMERICAN ARMY AIR SERVICE)

to DATE as such from the TWENTY-THIRD day of AUGUST nineteen hundred and NINETY-FOUR. This officer will therefore carefully and diligently discharge the duties of the office to which appointed by doing and performing all manner of things thereunto belonging:

And I do strictly charge and require those officers, and other personnel of lesser rank, to render such obedience as is due an officer of this grade and position. And this officer is to observe and follow such orders and directions, from time to time, as may be given by the President of the United States of America, or other superior officers acting in accordance with the laws of the United States of America.

This commission is to continue in force during the pleasure of the President of the United States of America, under the provisions of those public laws relating to Officers of the Armed Forces of the United States of America and the component thereof in which this appointment is made.

Done at the City of Washington, this FOURTEENTH day of SEPTEMBER in the year of our Lord, one thousand nine hundred and NINETY-FOUR, and of the Independence of the United States of America, the TWO HUNDRETH.

By the President:

Lieutenant General, USAF
Deputy Chief of Staff, Personnel

Secretary of the Air Force

This commission, signed by the Secretary of the Air Force and the USAF Deputy Chief of Staff in 1994, posthumously promoted Bullard to second lieutenant in the United States Air Force.

French Pronunciation Guide

Angoulême	ahn[1] goo-LEM
Arc de Triomphe	ark duh tree-OHMF
Arras	ah-RAH
Artois Ridge	ar-TWAH
Avenue du Bois de Boulogne	ah-vuh-NYEW dyew bwa duh boo-LOAN-yuh
Avord	ah-VOR
Bar-le-Duc	bar-luh-DYUKE
Bastille	bah-STEE-yuh
Beau-Zie-sur-Aire	bow ZEE see-ur AIR
Bethonsart	bay-ton[1] ZAR
Biarritz	bee-ar-REETZ
Blériot	blair-ee-OH
Bordeaux	bor DOH
Boulevard Montparnasse	bool-VAR mon[1] par-NAHS
Brun	bruhn[5]
Café du Commerce	cah-FAY dyu coe-MAIRS
Calais	cah LAY
Caudron	coe-DRON[1]
Caz-au-lac	cahz-oh-LAHK
Chalons-sur-Marne	shah-LON syoor MARN

Champagne	shahm PAH nyuh
Chartres	SHAR truh
Châteauroux	chat-TOH-ROO
Chevert	shuh-VAIR
Chevillard	shuh-vee-YAR
Commandant Ménard	coe-mahn[2] DAHN[2] may-NAR
Croix de Guerre	cwah duh GAIR
Douaument	doo-ah-MAHN[2]
Elysées Montmarte	ay-lee-ZAY mon[1] MAR-truh
Fleury	flur-REE
Fontaine du Berger	fone TEN dyoo bear ZHAY[3]
Fourragere	foo-rah-ZHAIR[3]
George	zhorzh[3]
Givery-en-Argonne	zhee[3] vair EE en[2] ar-GOAN
Hendaye	en[2] DIE
Hotel Dieu	oh-TELL DYUH
Jacques	ZHAHK[3]
Képi	kay-PEE
L'Escadrille	les-cwah-DREE-yuh
La Rotonde	lah ro-TOHN[1] duh
Le Blanc	luh BLAHN[2]
Le Grand Duc	luh grahn[2] DYUKE
La Marseillaise	lah mar-say-YEZ
Le Plessis Belleville	luh pleh-SEE bell-VEEL

Leplanquais	luh-plahn[2] KAY
Lyons	lee-ON[1]
Madame Nesmé	mah-DAHM nez-MAY
Mêlée	muh-LAY
Merci, madame	mair-SEE mah-DAHM
Mon ami	moan ah-MEE
mon Commandant	mon[1] com[1] mahn[2] DAHN[2]
Monsieur	miss see UR
Mont-Saint-Eloi	mon[1] SANT[4] el-oo-WAH
Moronvilliers Hills	mon[1] ron[1] vee-lee-AY
Navarin Farm	nah-vah-RAN[4]
Neuilly	nuh YEE
Nieuport	nyuh-POR
Non, mon capitain	non[1] mon[1] cah-pee-TAN[4]
Nouvion	noo-vee-ON[1]
Orléans	or lay AHN[2]
Oui	oo-WEE
Paleolouge	pah lay oh LOHG
Pisard	pee ZAR
Place des Armes	plahs days ARM
Porte D'Italie	por dee-tahl-LEE
Rendevous	ran[2] day-VOO
River Aisne	ehznuh
Roleur	roo-LUR

Sacré bleu	sah-cray BLUH
Somme	sum
Somme-py	sum-PEE
Souain-en-Champagne	soo- AN[4] en[2] shahm-PAH-nyuh
Souchez	soo-SHAY
St. Jean de Luz	san[4] zhan[3] duh LEWS
Suippes	sweep
Tourelles	too-RELL
Trés bien	treh bee-AN[4]
Vadalaincourt	vah-dah-lan[4] COOR
Vaux	voh
Vermouth cassis	vair-MOOT cah-SEE
Vive la France	VEEV lah FRANS[2]
Vive la Légion	VEEV lah lay-zhee[3] ON[1]
Vouziers	voo-zee-AY

[1] "on" as the "o" in "only" (the "n" is NOT pronounced)
[2] "en" as in "entrée" (the "n" is NOT pronounced)
[3] "j" sounds like the "s" in "measure"
[4] "a" as in "and"
[5] "u" as in "under" (the "n" is NOT pronounced)

Further Reading

Carisella, P. J., James W. Ryan and Edward W. Brooke. *The Black Swallow of Death: The Incredible Story of Eugene Jacques Bullard, The World's First Black Combat Aviator.* Boston: Marlborough House, 1972.

Lloyd, Craig. *Eugene Bullard: Black Expatriate in Jazz Age Paris.* Athens: University of Georgia Press, 2000.

Mason, Herbert Molloy, Jr. *High Flew the Falcons: The French Aces of World War I.* New York: J. B. Lippincott, 1965.

Nordhoff, Charles and James Norman Hall. *The Lafayette Flying Corps.* Boston and New York: Houghton Mifflin, 1920.

Shack, William A. *Harlem in Montmarte: A Paris Jazz Story Between the Great Wars.* Berkeley: University of California Press, 2001.

Index